CastOff

CastOff

True Adventures and Ordeals
of an American Family on a French Farm

Jan Murra

New Horizon Press
Far Hills, New Jersey

New Horizon Press
P.O. Box 669
Far Hills, NJ 07931

Murra, Jan
    CastOff: True Adventures and Ordeals of an American
    Family on a French Farm

Illustrations: JoAnn DeSnyder Rolfe
Interior Design: Susan M. Sanderson

Library of Congress Control Number: 2001089171

ISBN: 0-88282-209-8
New Horizon Press

Manufactured in the U.S.A.

2006   2005   2004   2003   2002   /   5   4   3   2   1

Cast off
Let go; set loose
American Heritage Dictionary

Cast off
To reject
American Heritage Dictionary

Now it is high time to awake out of sleep:
For now is our salvation, nearer than when we believed.
The night is far spent, the day is at hand: let us therefore
***Cast off** the works of darkness and let us put on the armor*
of light.

Romans, Chapter 13, Verses 11 & 12

Cast off
Undo mooring lines in
preparation of departure
Nautical Dictionary

Cast off
To throw away or aside
Merriam-Webster's Collegiate Dictionary

Acknowledgements

To my mentors and friends, Maralys Wills and Paul Morris, for their guidance and encouragement.

To my children and best beloveds, Wendy, Dan, Tim and Jill, for sharing their lives with me.

To my husband, Dick, for his unfailing love and support.

And, finally, credit must be given to my once-husband, Rob, for dumping us on an antiquated farm in southwestern France, without which we would not have had the empowering, enriching and adventurous experiences of our decade on *Vezat* and this book would never have been written.

Contents

∾ PART 1 ∾

Cherchant Le Rêve

Undimmed by city lights,
patterns of the night sky
spin in silent orbits,
shimmering—still.

Patterns of the night sky
pass over the farm on the hill,
shimmering—still,
devoid of claxon, clanging, calling.

Passing over the farm on the hill
tranquil—darkly,
devoid of claxon, clanging, calling,
bounding with life, spirit, zest.

Tranquil—darkly,
only the soft pad of night creatures

bounding with life, spirit, zest,
the shush of cattle ruminating.

Only the soft pad of night creatures
communing with the stars,
the shush of cattle ruminating,
the heartbeat of peace.

Communing with the stars
spinning in silent orbit.
The heartbeat of peace,
undimmed by city lights.

❧ CHAPTER 1 ❧

Just Another Saturday

It was a Saturday, just like any other Saturday, the day my life turned upside down. Rob, my husband, had gone to his office, even though he had completed most of the paperwork selling his half of a partnership in a small stock brokerage firm. He was a workaholic in every sense of the word, particularly since the noisy play of our four children, all under the age of eleven, along with assorted neighborhood kids and friends, kept the house from settling too firmly on its foundations. Working kept him out of the turmoil.

"I won't be home late, promise. Maybe we can barbecue this evening. Bye, kids. Bye, Jan. Be good." He planted a kiss somewhere near my lips and was out the door.

"Hey, Dad, you gonna catch my game?" Nine-year-old Danny ran in, mitt on one hand and bat and ball in the other. "Coach said I could pitch today." Baseball and Little League were his life and, all motherly modesty aside, the kid was good. Hey, it wasn't me throwing that little white ball.

"I'll try, son. Gotta go." The door slammed behind him.

The television in the family room blared out Spider-man's latest epic achievement. The two youngest, Jill, five, and Timmy, seven, still in pajamas with jelly mustaches from morning toast adorning their faces, were raptly absorbed in making a tent from the coffee table to the couch using a sheet dragged from the clean-but-unfolded laundry pile. Danny had raced outdoors with bat, ball and glove yelling for the neighbor kids and hoping to get a game started. Weekends and school holidays were one long game. Rainy days were hell.

I plopped a load of sheets into an overworked washing machine, added soap powder, prayed it would cooperate and pushed the switch, then shooed our big tiger cat out of the dryer and grabbed a warm armful of jeans and sweatshirts to dump on the dining room table for folding. Ironing, in our house, was an unheard-of luxury. Just getting the clothes folded and put away was barely possible.

While I folded and stacked, I mentally calculated the day's activities. Little League at eleven and it was my turn to carpool a bunch (a herd? a gaggle? a mess?) of boys. Our older daughter Wendy was due at Melinda's before noon for a day of pre-teen girls, giggles and horses followed by a slumber party. An oxymoron if I ever heard one! Wendy's horse, Candy, was a sweet natured, 4-H trained pinto who had lived in our garage until she knocked the glass out of the window and door and was now boarded in a barn at Wendy's friend Melinda's house.

We lived in a two-story clapboard house painted white with blue shutters sitting on an acre of wooded land in the part of New Jersey for which the Garden State was named. The neighborhood was restricted to acre lot minimums and many homes had horses pastured alongside.

"Mom, my fish looks funny. D'you think he's dead?" Wendy yelled from the second floor. Grabbing a pile of folded towels, I headed up the stairs and into her room, which gurgled and bubbled with the sounds of a tropical fish tank. Reflected aqueous flickers gave the impression of stepping into an underwater kingdom.

Walking over to it, I peered at the fish floating on the surface of the tank. "Kind of looks that way. I'm sorry, honey." I set the towels on the bed and picked up the scooper net.

"Now the other kissing gourami won't have anyone to kiss," Wendy said sorrowfully then ran to the head of the stairs, yelling, "Tim, Jill, come on up. Fish funeral!"

The four of us gathered around the toilet, fish net poised above the tank as Wendy solemnly intoned, "I consign you to the deep. May God have mercy on your soul." I flipped the tiny creature into the water, she pushed the handle and with a gurgle and swish it was gone as Tim and Jill applauded. I really hoped my own soul wasn't being consigned to perdition for this heresy. God only knew where Wendy got her script for these funeral services.

"Okay, guys, time to get washed and dressed." And another day was off and running.

When we arrived home mid-afternoon after the game, with a stopover at Dairy Queen for treats all-round in celebration of Danny's winning home run, Rob was already there. *Great*, I thought. *Maybe that barbecue would be a go after all.*

He shipped the boisterous boys along with Jill out to the backyard and poured me an ice cold beer. After fourteen years of marriage, he still had that clean-cut, boy-next-door look and grinning imps danced in his hazel eyes. Always my downfall.

"You'll never guess who I talked with today," he said. "Bernard Benson."

I shuddered. Our ex-boss from California was nuts. I mean he was certifiable. Quite possibly a genius, sometimes even a nice guy, but the man was crazy as a loon. He was a round man with hair that looked as if he had just been zapped with multiple kilovolts of electricity. Come to think of it, he could have passed for Albert Einstein, in more ways than hair.

"What a great idea!" Rob said, bouncing around the room enthusiastically. I realized I'd missed part of the conversation as I was mentally conjuring Bernard Benson.

"What's a great idea?" If Bernard had anything to do with it, I wasn't at all sure I'd agree to its greatness.

"He's bought a castle in France and moved the family over. Says it's fantastic for the kids. No drugs, great schools and simple country living. Said we'd love it. How would you like to move over there?"

"You must be kidding." I stared at him in horror. It was one thing to dream of castles in France. Quite another to consider seriously packing up bag and baggage and kids and dogs, maybe even a horse, and transplanting us. They spoke a different language, one that none of us knew. Schools might be a challenge. Hell, living would be a challenge.

As I said, Bernard was nuts. He was also half-French and spoke the language. He'd sold his company of peripheral computer equipment a few years back and made a small fortune. Actually, a good-sized one. Enough to buy an honest-to-goodness castle in France and pack off his entire family: wife, seven kids, plus a few dogs and several horses.

I shrugged my shoulders uncertainly and studied my husband. Rob had recently taken his computer services company public and then sold his shares to his partner. With the proceeds he started a stock brokerage firm and bought a seat on the National Stock Exchange. Then, when the market turned downward, he sold that to another partner and retained a small, struggling printing company, hoping for a stock offering in a waning market.

He did well on all these transactions, but I wouldn't exactly call it a fortune, not even a small one. What Rob really needed, I felt, was a regular job with regular hours.

To follow my husband's pursuit of his objectives, our four children, with but six years between the oldest and youngest, were born in three different states at opposite ends of the country. Since our marriage, we'd lived in nine houses in four states. And Rob wasn't even in the military. I referred to him as a professional gypsy.

Rob had a sincere charm, the sort of man any mother would instantly trust with her daughter. Great sense of humor but with a serious side. Men were drawn to his technical expertise in the dawning field of computers as well as to his liberal hand at the bar. Women were attracted to the laughing adventurer. I thought we were soul-mates and fiercely refused to question the reason behind his many extended trips to Washington. His explanations were always so clear, so reasonable.

The children went to good schools and were all excellent students. Wendy, small and blonde, was serious and bright and her life centered around her horse. Danny, the only dark-haired one in a family of towheads, was intense. Timmy, with his fair shaggy mop, had a special sweetness to his nature and an affinity for needing hospital emergency rooms. I often wondered what would have held him together had catgut not existed. Angelic-faced Jill, not yet in kindergarten, was still considered to be the baby of the family. Most of the time her boisterous, outgoing siblings were simply too much for her.

I was a Girl Scout leader and directed two handbell choirs at St. John's Methodist Church. We had a choice of two baby-sitters, both of whom ranked right up there with Mary Poppins, within walking distance. Our lives were full and complete, but as the children grew older, I was starting to fear the menace of drugs and violence rampant in our culture.

Rob seemed to fear them too.

"Just as soon as I can improve the printing company's balance sheet, we'll take it public. It should be really hot and we'll make a mint and then we'll show those French how to farm. In the meantime, you can get the kids settled in their new French school." Rob's eyes had never been more sincere. "Bernard says household help is cheap. How'd you like a French cook?"

My eyes widened. He was talking as if moving to another continent were more than just a daydream. What I really wanted was a full-time husband, this one. If he weren't away so much, not stressed with business concerns, I thought, we could be a couple again, a family again. I stared at Rob and began envisioning a different atmosphere, a renewed relationship. A continent away from the big attraction in Washington. Maybe this would do it. Just maybe.

Before I knew what hit me, the decision was made and furniture was walking out of the house with new owners. I said good-bye to my beloved spinet piano, bought by my parents when I was five, my mother's glass-doored china cupboard along with beds, dressers, you-name-it. A few months later, we were spending our last night in our wooded home in sleeping bags on the floor.

I was excited and scared. Adventure sat at my door beckoning and I knew I was on the verge of obeying its call. Still, fears bubbled up within me. I wasn't terrified for myself, but we were taking four young children into an unknown world, trusting their fates and futures to God-knew-what. They weren't terribly pleased about our plan to relocate, which meant leaving everything and everyone they knew for a strange and foreign world. I had to be constantly upbeat and positive to counteract their reluctance and, at times, outright rebellion. And I prayed quietly that we were doing the right thing.

Wendy agreed to sell her horse only upon receiving an IOU signed in blood that she would have another immediately upon arrival at her new home. I didn't mention that her dad had been giving me blank checks with a picture of a horse in the amount space for every one of my birthdays for the past thirteen years, ever since my adored quarterhorse, Flash, had to be put down shortly after our marriage. Promises are easy to make, but the reasons for not fulfilling them come even easier.

CHAPTER 2

Vacationing Canines

We didn't just move the immediate family, we moved like the ancient Egyptians were buried, complete with the family pets. This was, actually, a necessity if we wanted the children to accompany us. They refused to leave without our dogs.

We had two canine pets: Penny, a fat black Labrador and Schultz, a loyal, slightly schizo dachshund who knew when to sit up and be cute and when to make himself scarce—valuable traits in a dog. Both dogs had been well trained to sit quietly under the table and eat the children's rejects. Unfortunately for the kids, the dogs didn't much like green vegetables either.

Our familial move to France was done in groups, the purpose of this being that the first ones to arrive could set up a spot where the dogs would be accepted until we found our eventual home. In hindsight, it seems to me that there are several more rational methods, like finding the eventual home to begin with.

Anyway, Danny, Jill and I were the first to arrive in Marseilles and, as soon as we rented a small villa for a couple of weeks, we wired the others to send the dogs. Two days later, at the airport, we awaited the scheduled arrival of our canine freight. The plane landed, we paced and dithered around the baggage area...and waited...and paced...and waited some more. No dogs. None.

Seeing a distressed, just turned six-year-old with tears dripping off her chin and a ten-year old boy fighting a quivering lip, two sympathetic baggage handlers came over to see if they could help. I pulled together my limited knowledge of the language and asked brightly about our pets: "No *chiens*?" I slowly shook my head to accentuate my attempt at communication.

"*Non, il n'y a pas de chiens,*" they responded firmly.

That seemed to cover the situation, but we were still distressed and they were curious.

"*Vous êtes en vacances?*" they asked.

"*Oui,*" I answered. Not knowing the words to express that we weren't actually on vacation, but in the process of moving, I simply took the easy way out. In cases like this, it's simpler to agree.

They looked at each other and then back at the crazy Americans who would take pets along on a holiday abroad.

"*Les chiens aussi?*" They smiled with this final proof of our instability. Only the truly insane, and those with more money than common sense, take their dogs on vacations 3,000 miles from home.

Jill, Danny and I met every plane from Paris that neverending day. Each time, our friendly baggage handlers came out sadly shaking their heads, "*Pas de chiens.*"

Little Jill's tears were flowing freely and Danny was having a real problem retaining his manly stoicism. Toward evening the dogs were discovered, debarked in Paris, but not yet placed on a connecting flight to Marseilles. We were told this would most likely occur during the night or in the early morning hours. Our kindly baggage men suggested that I take the children home, to our "vacation" home, insisting with many gestures and pantomime that they would telephone the number I jotted down for them as soon as the dogs arrived.

We drooped with fatigue and discouragement and tried to hide the fear we felt for our pets, whom we pictured cowering in their kennels, shivering in terror and suffering pangs of hunger and thirst. In fact, we later learned, they were dining in Paris on *steak aux poivre* without, of course, *le vin rouge* and being petted and pampered by half of Air France's staff. The dogs may not have understood the language, but gourmet fare and kindness are universal. Not knowing our pets were living it up in style, we drove to our little villa, made sandwiches which we tried, without much luck, to swallow through the lumps in our throats and went to bed.

The morning sun was igniting the uppermost tip of the fig tree outside our windows after a night spent dreaming of the dogs, one clinging to each wing of a plane while the Red Baron, scarf streaming in the wind, swooped across the sky, when the phone rang. As I stumbled across the room, I had a moment's panic wondering how I would understand without the visual images and pantomimes. I needn't have worried. A tired, but delighted baggage handler, who had stayed at his post well beyond his usual shift, barked joyously, "*Woof! woof! Les chiens sont la—woof! woof! woof!*"

We drove to the airport in record time and raced to the baggage area to be greeted by two ecstatic dogs. Our new French friends smiled as they watched the children kissing and hugging the dogs and running in total abandon around the area, fortunately nearly deserted in the early morning hour. As I made out the requisite paperwork, the Frenchmen were telling everyone who passed by the story of *"les Americaines fous et les chiens en vacances."* The crazy Americans with their vacationing dogs.

The dogs were none the worse for their adventure. *Au contraire*, they were well-fed and rested. International travelers without jet lag. I, on the other hand, was cranky, sleep-deprived, hungry and thoroughly sick of Operation Let's-Move-to-a-Simpler-Life. *Simpler for whom?* I asked myself.

❧ CHAPTER 3 ❧

Searching for Oz

We stayed at the little walled villa in Cassis, a village outside Marseilles, for a month, long enough to acclimate the dogs and wait for Rob to arrive with Wendy and Tim. Finally the three of them flew to France by way of Germany and collected a Volkswagen minibus directly from the factory, then drove down the Autobahn and through France to Cassis.

When they arrived, we couldn't wait to show them the new sights and sounds of a French village and to show off our new knowledge of all things French. The Mediterranean with its iridescent blue water, heavenly to swim in, but with a beach composed of tiny, sharp rocks which required plastic sandals to avoid cutting tender toes; the village square in the evening filled with old men playing boules, a complex game with small steel balls involving much pacing and concentration and long silences punctuated by furiously shouted words we couldn't understand (probably a good thing); the pizza shop which sold pizzas unlike anything we'd ever tasted, topped with wrinkled vinegar-soaked olives, sardines and capers; the quantities of homeless cats we encountered on every walk lurking in the alleyways.

Trying to decide where to make our permanent home, Rob and I poured over maps.

I wasn't sure when or how he became an expert on the region, but he offered, "The South of France would be perfect. The weather is mild year-round. You and the kids would love that, wouldn't you?"

Shocked, I looked up at him. "What do you mean, me and the kids? You'll be here too, won't you?"

He flushed. "Of course. I'm talking now, getting settled, you know. I still have to get the printing company on its feet before it can be sold."

We headed north from Marseilles, like pioneers, the VW loaded with luggage, kids, food for picnics along the way and dogs. Penny wasn't a good traveler and worried a lot, so she sat in the space between the driver's and front passenger's seats and drooled incessantly, creating a small lake which flowed back and forth with the tilt of the car.

"Oooooh, gross! Mom, can't you do something about her?" I don't know what they expected. A bib perhaps?!

Erma Bombeck had the right idea when she said that one should never have more kids than the car has windows. The bus satisfied that condition, but unfortunately, they were still close enough to touch each other, and as soon as boredom set in—about five minutes after ignition—the battles commenced.

"Mom, he's hogging Schultz. It's my turn. Tell him."

"Can't you tell him yourself?"

"She's touching me. Mom, make her stop!"

"I'm hungry."

"Are we there yet?"

"I have to pee."

And I had my own troubles. Rob had a tendency to leave the main road and head down village lanes, seeking the perfect spot to homestead. Then I had to consult the map and map-reading while driving tended to make me carsick and gave me a headache. As we drove on and on, I began to reflect that encountering Indians with bows and arrows was possibly a welcome respite to pioneer wives and mothers. At least it kept them from killing off family members themselves.

We stopped at small real estate offices along the way to view photos of picturesque cottages and sleek cows grazing in the pastures, models of bucolic tranquility. The farms in person, so to speak, were devoid of plumbing except for wells in the front yards and modern conveniences were remarkable for their absence. We soon found the charm was all on the outside; within there were bare walls and floors, simple tables and chairs, no built-in storage or closets, no countertops. Decorators' nightmares! The cottages, picturesque though they might be, sat on desolate ground and any tree brave enough to push its roots into the rocky soil, tilted drunkenly to the side in mute evidence of the mistral winds which roared through the Rhone Valley for months at a time. The properties were unbelievably remote.

I was becoming weary and discouraged from the search. "We might as well move to a deserted island. I didn't think the plan was to leave civilization entirely." My sense of adventure was stretching its limits.

Rob, however, still seemed charmed. "There was a village a few miles back," he insisted.

"We could build our own baseball diamond in that field." Danny still had his supply of bats, balls and gloves, ever-hopeful of bringing baseball to the underprivileged French. "But I don't see any kids around."

We passed through Arles and Avignon, traveling ever northward from the Bouches-du-Rhone, the Vaucluse, Drome. Tiny villages appeared in the windshield and disappeared via the rearview mirrors. We bought loaves of crusty bread, cheese and fruit along with bottles of wine and Orangina. We couldn't find milk and the kids were delighted. We felt terribly international and world travelerish.

Soon, however, another problem intervened.

"Mom, we have to stop. I WON'T pee behind a bush!" Wendy wasn't in to simple country living and her father, in common with many American males, hated losing precious travel time searching for gas stations. Then we discovered that French gas stations didn't come equipped with the uniquely American facility, the Clean Rest Room, which may be an oxymoron but nevertheless, comes in very handy.

"Oh for God's sake! If you've got to go, just go. We haven't seen another car in a hundred miles and there's a nice big bush over there." Patience wasn't Rob's strong point.

"Dad, I can't. And I REALLY have to go. Pleeeeeeeze."

In the next village we came to, we finally located a small café, dark and empty, but with the door open and an elderly woman counting change behind the counter. It had come as a surprise to us that every store in town closed down for two hours at lunch time and cafés closed between meal-times. She pointed to a door at the back and opening it, the girls and I saw a small hut. When we stepped inside, we found a hole in the floor with two foot-shaped blocks on either side. That was it.

Wendy stared in shock.

"Honey, I'm afraid this is the best we're going to get. You stand on the blocks, squat and pee. Or whatever. We're not in Kansas anymore." I giggled. As did Jill. Wendy didn't speak to us for miles.

We got on our way again and the afternoon slowly wore on. We were starting to feel a nip in the air and the Volkswagen's engine strained slightly up ever-steeper hills. A landscape in varying shades of brown turned to a vivid green liberally dotted with pastel wildflowers, a Laura Ashley vista. We'd arrived at the French Alps. Mountain peaks perpetually white capped reared over us, often shrouded in drifting clouds. After a long day driving, we pulled into a *pensione* in a charming chalet. Our hostess gave us mugs of creamy hot chocolate and chunks of warm bread and we crawled under thick, fluffy duvets and were immediately asleep.

Way too early in the morning, the sun barely sneaking peeks at the day, we awoke to the sound of bells, stomping hooves and rustles of hay, an occasional deep, male voice and the pungent aroma of cows. I stepped to the window, shivering as my bare feet touched the frigid floorboards. Our rooms were directly over the milking barn and our host was busily engaged in the morning chores.

Fortunately, we were the only guests and had the single bathroom down the hall to ourselves, although the supply of hot water ran out well before the number of baths.

That day we visited a chalet perched on the side of a hill. I use the word "hill" loosely. The hill was steep and high enough to make my ears pop and the VW throttle well down in first gear. Hairpin turns on the road were marked with curved mirrors planted to give a view of anything approaching around the bend, thus avoiding face to face confrontations in impossible situations. Despite the difficulty maneuvering, the view was spectacular. Even the perpetual argument from the back seats was temporarily silenced as the kids gazed in awe.

The chalet itself was quaint, charming. It even had indoor facilities. I felt like Gretel or perhaps Heidi. The day was clear, the air pristine if, perhaps, slightly rarified; musical bells from cattle grazing on the hillside rang gently in the distance. I'd heard that the farmers could tell if the herd was complete by the tones of the bells. The guiding agent on this tour spoke fair English, a fact for which I regularly uttered heartfelt thanks to my guardian angel. When I asked about winters, he pointed to the ski lift rising nearby and mentioned that the lift was the only means of access when snow was on the ground.

"*Les enfants* descend each morning and are picked up by bus for their school. *C'est très commode*, it is most convenient."

Rob turned to me. "What d'you think, honey? You could learn to ski. It's gorgeous here."

"Are you out of your cotton-picking mind?" I replied.

We said goodbye to the Alps and decided to head west. Rob's patience shortened as the time allotted for finding a place to live diminished. My mood wasn't exactly sunny either.

"I can't leave the company too long. There's so much to do," he grunted.

My voice became taut and cool. "I'm sorry we're such a burden. Maybe we should have planned ahead."

Tempers were stretched, fraying. To stop the friction, we tried to use the long hours of travel to peruse an old Elementary French book in order to learn numbers, some words and a few useful phrases.

We practiced our pronunciation. *"Garçon, la facture, s'il vous plaît."* After an hour, we could all ask the waiter for the bill. I didn't know how many times we would use our newly learned phrase, but at least we had it down pat.

As we drove westward toward the Dordogne region, the barren plains and windswept hills of the Camarque and the cloud-covered peaks of the Alps disappeared behind us. We entered a country of fertile green fields, grazing cattle and sheep, stone houses and barns roofed with slabs of stone or brick tiles. We passed medieval stone churches, ancient, fortified *chateaux* in ruins and others magnificently restored with circular towers and crenellated walls, meandering rivers arched by stone bridges and ancient mills still turning in the waters. We saw a village built into limestone cliffs rising from the banks of a river and tiny stone huts built by the ancient Gauls in the days of the Romans.

By the time we reached the *département* of the Dordogne, a portion of which was historically known as the Perigord and had its capital at the city of Perigueux, rain was falling steadily, cutting the view to little beyond the windshield wipers. The Dordogne is one of the most interesting regions of France, spectacularly beautiful with numerous rivers, forests, limestone cliffs, caves and plateaus. Its man-made attractions include prehistoric cave drawings, huge castles and chateaux and medieval walled bastions. I hoped the weather cleared soon, so we could better appreciate this paradise that lay just three hundred miles from Paris.

We came to the medieval city of Sarlat, built on the site of the Sarlat Monastery in 720 A.D. by the Benedictine Monks. We felt like time-travelers as we drove through narrow, cobblestone, winding streets bordered by perfectly preserved, richly ornamented seventeenth century and Renaissance buildings. Through archways, we caught glimpses of ancient courtyards. Thoroughly charmed, despite the bad weather, we had just about decided to pack it in for the night and find a place to stay when we saw a real estate office.

"There's still plenty of time to see something, even if it is raining. Let's stop," Rob said soberly.

Inside the office, a wizened old man sat behind the desk looking purposeful as he suggested a number of available properties to visit. He insisted we go to see them right away, especially one he was sure would be perfect for us, before they were snapped up by others whose arrival in the otherwise somnolent and empty office, he prophesied, was imminent.

❦ CHAPTER 4 ❧

Vezat

The *agent immobilière* (real estate agent) insisted on driving us, so we piled into his car and he, driving faster than appropriate, rushed us toward the appointed spot. We drove into a central courtyard with a large hay barn on one side and an even longer building, half the length of a football field, on the other. Both buildings were constructed with huge rocks that appeared to have been stuck together with gobs of mud. In places, the mud had dried up and fallen out, but the rocks stayed put by virtue of their own weight.

Vezat had magic. It was not immediately apparent, you understand, but there was a pervasive enchantment. That and a whole lot of cow dung.

Vezat is a fifty-acre farm located near the village of Saint-Cyprien in southwestern France. Before bringing us to the farm, the *agent* had shown us Saint-Cyprien, which spreads over a hillside on the right bank of the Dordogne

River. The village is dominated by a massive church, dedi-
cated to the saint who founded the village in the sixth century and belonging to the Augustinian Order. What is left
from time past is a sturdy-looking, Romanesque belfry-keep
from the twelfth century and the restored Gothic main body
of the church built in the fourteenth century. Handsome
stone houses, their slate or tile roofs sharply pitched, sur-
round the church on steep, narrow streets.

You can't get to the village from the United States
without taking a minimum of three different means of trans-
portation: plane, train and finally car or bicycle or moped or
whatever. Farms in that part of the world don't have
addresses, they have names. Finding them is your problem.

The magic wasn't evident at our first view. Every angel
in the heavens was sobbing, puddle by puddle, along with a
few devils. I say devils because some of that water clearly had
to have oozed up from below in order to create so much
mud. Our first step out of the car landed us knee deep in
muck.

Water dripped off my eyelashes and around my nos-
trils as I sloshed over and peered into the ancient barns.
Inside they were stuffed to the rafters with decades-old cow
dung and piles of dusty straw filled with mouse nests and
heaven-knows-what. The living quarters were contained in
one end of the long building, which also housed the animal
barns, giving family togetherness a whole new meaning and
were distinguished as a residence for humans by having glass
in the windows. The heavy wood door to the human living
quarters grumbled open like a waking bear, revealing mammoth beams coated with soot and festooned with spider web

subdivisions, a fireplace large enough for entire family gatherings and—no, I'm not kidding—a stone sink with a drain pipe leading to a hole in the outside wall.

"*Regardez lá!*" Back in the courtyard, the *agent immobilière* danced around us, pointing out the attributes of the farm; somehow his shiny black shoes never touched the mud and with his total supply of English words limited to ten, pointed with ecstasy to the new roof on the hay barn. "*Que c'est magnifique!*"

He couldn't seem to understand my question about the condition of the roof of the house, which appeared to be original issue, dating back at least 300 years. He spoke only to my husband. It was obvious to his way of thinking, women had two purposes, one of which was cooking and neither was decision-making. He jabbered on with wide sweeping gestures toward the old stone buildings and the fields obscured behind a curtain of rain, at times kissing his fingertips and extending his arms to the heavens as if imploring divine witness to the magnificence of the ancient farm. I couldn't understand a word. He might have been comparing our intelligence levels unfavorably with jungle baboons and discussing unsavory sexual practices of our parents, but, spoken in French, it sure sounded pretty.

Slogging through mud and peering through grime-caked windows, I failed to see any signs of plumbing nor did I detect any electric wires connecting to the buildings. I doubted there were underground utilities! My questions on these topics also fell on uncomprehending ears as the *agent* directed my husband's enthusiastic attention to an ancient bread oven attached to the barn. *Encroyable!* An appliance!

Rounding up the boys, who were off swinging on the beams and acquiring a coating of century-old dirt and what-not (don't ask) along with mud to the earlobes, we joined Wendy and Jill, who sat unhappily in the car pleading to "just leave this awful place."

When my husband turned the conversation toward price, contract terms and conversions of dollars to francs, our *agent's* working knowledge of the English language improved considerably. In fact, by the time the two men had reached an agreement, in front of, during and in spite of my appalled protestations, the *agent's* English was fluent and nearly accent-free.

"Sign here and here and when your check clears, the farm is yours. Good luck!" The agreement was signed in his office and we departed with fervent handshakes, barely escaping the traditional French cheek-kissing and his exclamations of "*Bonne chance!*" Good luck indeed!

This was the place, I kept telling myself, where our four children would learn the joys of a more simple life, far from the drugs, guns and gangs so prevalent in our own society. At least that was the bright idea that had convinced me of the wisdom of this precarious move.

I had a newfound respect for the pioneer women of America who left their comfortable homes to travel across the mountains and plains and start all over again. I'd always believed they were missing a few screws in the grey matter to go in the first place, but I appeared to have fallen for a similar line. I guess my modern grey matter was even less well equipped with the proper hardware.

When we next saw *Vezat*, the sun had reappeared and the mud had dried and we gazed across washed and sparkling fields and woods to the river winding through the valley below. The air was fragrant with well-bathed clover grass and apple blossoms. A pair of pheasants flushed with a beat of russet wings and droplets of dew glistened on the grass and leaves like an iridescent Milky Way.

That was when our fate was sealed.

∾ CHAPTER 5 ∾

Feline Squatter

Taking possession of the property wasn't quite as simple as the *agent* had intimated, of course. In France, bureaucracy often rules. The *agent* had to contact the *notaire*, who handled all legal and contractual matters involved in real estate transactions. The *notaire* had to contact the owner who was, apparently, in residence in Belgium. He, in turn, had to contact the *agent* who, again, contacted the *notaire* who would, *eventuellement*, get back to us. All of these contacts were done in quadruplicate with copies of everything being filed at the *mairie*, signed by everyone involved plus a few dozen other citizens just to make sure no one got left out. If so much as a comma was questioned on any document, it needed to make the rounds again for approval by all concerned. A lot of long-term job security was involved here.

By the time everyone was satisfied that the buyer really wanted to sell and at what price and that we really wanted to buy and that the price we were prepared to pay would cover the buyer plus sufficient *en plus* for the *agent*, the *notaire* and, I'm convinced, a number of other palms, enough time had passed that our household had increased by two cats who spoke the local language, Minette and Caramel, and a pair of rabbits. We really needed the room.

Since the sum total of our worldly goods comprised the clothes on our backs and in our suitcases, moving in involved buying some beds, linens, a camp stove, cooking pots and dishes. Rob whisked through to sign the endless papers, deposit us in our newly acquired stone ruins with a few sticks of furniture, kerosene lamps and promises to return. I know I detected a sigh of relief when he left for the airport with promises to be back as soon as possible. And then—there we were. The Simple Life was all around us, enveloped in spider webs and dried mud and with a few strange cows wandering around the fields.

I can't remember ever working so hard at cleaning, with so little effect. Our new home defied us all the way. The old house consisted of three rooms, two with wide plank floors that we swept and scrubbed. The third, which would serve as kitchen, was stone floored, with rounded indentations and ancient paw tracks. In stone? Curiouser and curiouser.

We dragged in an old wooden table, no veneer here, just thick, solid oak that must have weighed 200 pounds, found in one of the barns. One end of the table served as kitchen cupboard for stacking our supply of dishes and cooking utensils, the other for eating.

Windows were set into openings in the stone walls, which were at least three-feet thick. The mud packing between the stones was the consistency of concrete, except for those areas in which it had disintegrated and allowed wind and dust to blow through freely. Fortunately, since it was summer the air was relatively balmy. I prayed that winters in the Dordogne wouldn't be too severe.

One of our first chores was to make the barns usable by removing the head-high piles of dirty hay and whatnot. Locating some old pitchforks and shovels in the hay barn, the kids and I set to work in the smallest of the stables, thinking that it might be nice to be able to point with pride to at least one clean area before tackling the bigger ones. Sort of a policy of success breeding success.

It was a fine example of a summer day in the south of France. The sun was shining in a blue sky overhead as birds twittered in the trees, calling their friends to check out the crazy Americans. The children and I started with a great deal of enthusiasm, no skill and city slicker hands that formed blisters upon contact with the pitchforks. Enthusiasm dwindled rapidly, to be replaced by complaints and muttered groans of "child abuse," along with huge bouts of sneezing brought about by the release of clouds of dust and hay.

After an eternity of shoveling and hauling, we reached ground level and discovered a pile of old burlap bags containing the remnants of some long ago grain. When I reached into the pile to grab one of the bags, its rotting fibers collapsed and the contents tumbled out in a dusty, smelly, skittering mess. Skittering? "Oh my God!" I yelled. They really were skittering, mice of all sizes running in every direction.

The girls screamed and ran. The boys hollered and whomped the ground with their shovels. I yelled, "Get the cats!" Minette and Caramel were fetched and showed interest in the mice. Unfortunately, they were not interested in them as meals, but rather as a wonderful new game. Catch a mouse and then play with it. One. At a time. For as long as it will play. With the quantity of mice we had, I decided, they would have game material for the next fifty years.

Then I realized that another player had entered the arena and was neatly taking care of the problem. Schultz, the dachshund, had heard the commotion and ambled in. Although he didn't know it, generations of ratting had been bred into his blood and bones. He instinctively set about doing what came naturally. For Schultz, this didn't involve playing around. A quick snap of the jaws, a toss of his head and, within minutes, the carnage was complete. Soon there wasn't a critter moving inside the barn except for a pair of highly annoyed cats looking for another game and Schultz, at point and alert.

My daughters had departed the war zone in disgust and flatly refused to return. The boys and I prodded cautiously around in the remaining hay, but nothing bounded out except billows of dust and dirt. We decided to give our throbbing hands a break and check the bigger stable area next door to assess the situation there.

Moments later we saw that this part of the barn was higher and extended farther back into the hillside. Wooden shutters on a large, high window at the back hung askew, allowing the sun's rays to filter through accumulated dust and cobwebs. Huge oak beams traversed the barn, cut from ancient forest behemoths, and from the top of one gleamed two wary golden eyes. An enormous black and white cat sat so still we looked directly at her for several minutes before realizing she was real. She was still hoping for invisibility.

I sent Danny to the kitchen for a small bowl of milk and in that second of shifting my eyes from the beam, the cat disappeared. We set the bowl to the side of the big front double doors, gazed for a moment on a mucking-out job of mammoth proportions and left the occupant in peace, closing the doors behind us.

During the next few days, the milk disappeared with regularity, as did any milk-soaked bread or cooked rice left over from meals prepared for the other spoiled members of the household. The days of buying commercial varieties of dog or cat foods were over. Those items in the local *épicerie* were rare and prohibitively expensive, carried only for tourists. Way beyond our means. Our animals survived, nay thrived, on diets of powdered milk mixed with whole-grain breads or rice bought at the local farm co-op and cooked with butcher's scraps and leftovers from the human table.

The black and white cat, ChiChi—all the animals received names whether they recognized them or not and, in ChiChi's case, she didn't recognize us, much less a name—remained invisible. If not for the disappearing food, we would have begun to doubt we'd ever laid eyes on her. Then one day a few weeks later, Tim climbed to the outside of the window at the back of the big barn and peered in. His eyes adjusted slowly to the dim, dusty light of the interior. At that point, he got so excited he lost his precarious hold, thudded to the ground and raced around to the kitchen, yelling, "She's got kittens, Mom. She's got kittens!"

It required all my powers of persuasion to convey to the kids that these were actually wild animals and to restrain the entire crew from rushing the barn. Persuasion followed

by firm dictatorial edicts. "No, you will NOT go in the barn.
Leave them in peace. Eventually—maybe—they'll learn that we
bring food and are not dangerous."

As the kittens grew, they ventured farther and farther
from the nest, even at times slipping under the big double
barn doors to take peeks at the wide world beyond. If one of
the dogs had the misfortune to choose that time to amble
through the courtyard, he risked a slashing attack from a
black-and-white blur, leaving his tender nose dripping blood.

With the perpetual threat of crossing ChiChi's path
hanging over their heads, both dogs ceased their patrols of
the central courtyard and their playful pounces on passing
poultry. The chickens re-grew their tail feathers and the dogs
became haunted beasts, moving from one end of the building
to the other by slinking furtively around the back and nudging open the door at the other end. Now that they were aware
of the arsenal of weapons available to felines, even our sleek,
lazy cats received new levels of respect.

ChiChi eventually accepted our presence as well as
our food, although we never for an instant believed that the
farm belonged more to us than to her. In her case, she was
there first and firmly believed in the principle that possession is nine-tenths of the law. She never came close enough to
be touched, but often sat in the courtyard to bathe in the sun
and supervise her small family. The kittens, on the other
hand, turned out to be wholly corruptible, playing with the
children and accepting their caresses. None would, however,
enter our living quarters. All contact remained in the open,
on their territory and on their terms.

During that period, I spent many midnight hours sitting
in an open field propped by an ancient oak while the cows

placidly chewed their cuds under stars captured in the tree-tops. An occasional flare whizzed across the black expanse to disappear into nothing. Bemoaning the relative ease of my suburban housewife past and bewailing the outrageous fortune which landed me in my current existence, I bitched and wept to the compassionate beasts. They munched. I bellyached. They chewed. I sobbed.

Soon I realized that the basis for therapy dispensed by the beasts and the fields worked something like this: give the human a full load of new problems and there's little time left to fret about the old ones. That and enough sheer physical labor to render a body so tired that deep and dreamless sleep becomes inevitable. Sure beats the hell out of a psychiatrist's couch.

Along with the inexpressible peace of fields surrounded by ancient woods, guarded by a jillion stars, the only sounds being the placid munching of the cows and an occasional "Who?" called softly from the trees.

❧ CHAPTER 6 ❧

Gabriel

Our *agent immobilière* had neglected to inform us of one rather significant fact regarding the property we had just purchased. Gabriel came with the farm. Sort of. Anyone leasing farm land in France has the right to continue the lease through the end of November of the year in which a property is sold, to complete the harvest. Since we bought *Vezat* in July, Gabriel became "our farmer" for the remainder of that year.

He strode into the courtyard, emerging from his rusty, clattering Renault one morning, deep set brown eyes grinning out from a weathered but attractive brown face, a faded black beret perched on wavy salt and pepper hair. Bouncing out the door behind him came a small black dog with tufted ears and a scruffy tail moving propeller fashion.

Soon I found out that Gabriel loved good wine. His eyes were never without their sparkle, the cheeks never less than blossoming.

To Gabriel, we were objects of curiosity pinned like butterflies to a board for his perusal. Americans were strange beings who bought new cars when the batteries of their old ones died. We'd bought a farm without a clue how to farm it. He found us an endless source of amusement.

Our limited textbook French fell far short of understanding his slurred mix of French and patois. Undeterred, he chuckled and tried with gestures and different words to gain our comprehension. Friendly and warm, he was, at best, a lackadaisical farmer, but a good teacher and he loved teaching us the trade since, knowing nothing, we were easily impressed with his expertise.

He had two fields planted, one in corn, the other in tobacco. His prayers wafted up daily to the rain gods to shower on the corn and help it thrive. Other supplications soared forth for swarms of locusts, fire or flood to shrivel the tobacco and zap it right off its sturdy roots. He could have cared less about protecting young lungs from the evils of nicotine. What counted was that the crop was insured by the government and he'd get paid whether it grew or not. Each day the tobacco continued to grow was a direct affront. And most likely the direct result of insurgent political activities of the Opposition Party.

Gabriel's vineyard, on the other hand, was a labor of love. Each vine was laboriously tended. No mother's hands could be more tender than Gabriel's in probing the leaves for signs of hungry green worms. No weed dared poke its head up between the rows. Branches were tied to wires strung tautly between posts planted firmly at each row. The result was a symphony of well-mannered plants, bearing bunches of ripening fruits. Obviously loved, disciplined and lacking in neither attention nor concern. Nothing within his power would mar the success of the year's wine.

Gabriel also had half a dozen young heifers on the land that first summer and their regular sorties into the cornfield were due to the full moon, a battery failure in the electric fence or other happenings beyond his control, never a rickety fence line that he had failed to fortify. Many nights we were awakened by the sounds of cattle milling around in the courtyard and sleepily roused ourselves to push the stubborn beasts back into the pasture. In the morning, Gabriel chortled happily, cleaned up the mess, patched the fence with a bit of baling wire, then stopped by the kitchen for a glass (or two) of wine. I often thought we should plant some grapevines on the cattle fences, then, perhaps, they would get their fair share of attention.

One unforgettable August night, we were awakened sometime after midnight with enormous claps of thunder, flashes of lightning that illuminated the night sky like floodlights at a video store grand opening and gale force winds banging the wooden shutters against the stone building. Now we understood why the locals firmly closed and latched the shutters at night. Who knew?

We opened the windows wide. Tim balanced on the sill (fortunately those huge rocks made a good fulcrum point) and hung out while we clutched his legs to keep him from falling and splatting in the mud while he grabbed the shutters. This process unleashed the full force of the wind into the room, as well as letting in buckets of rain. We struggled as a group to pull the shutters closed as the wind did its best to foil the effort. Finally, the only window remaining with banging shutters was the one overlooking Gabriel's field of corn. This window faced directly into the wind, which whipped our hair and tried to snatch the eyelashes off our faces. Drenching rain was flung horizontally into the room. The dogs milled around us—wet, happy and underfoot. The cats, with far greater intelligence, burrowed under blankets deep into the beds.

The sky exploded with a momentary flash of brilliance and there, unfazed by the storm, enjoying a midnight snack of sweet green corn, were Gabriel's heifers. The kids muttered imprecations which I didn't know they understood, much less knew the French equivalents, and we pulled on jeans and shirts and headed out into the elements. I was compelled to admit that life at *Vezat* wasn't dull, even without television.

We spent the next half hour stumbling through head-high corn in pitch blackness, being rained on equally from the heavens and from the water jostled loose from the large flat leaves. Each crack of thunder was followed by yelps from the children and...yes, I admit it...from me. I was not a tower of strength. Occasional flashes of lightning often found one or more of us face to startled bovine face, which resulted in the cow dashing one way and human the other. It didn't take us long to realize that our discomfort was only surpassed by our ineffectiveness and we retreated to the house to dry ourselves off, compare stories and retire to bed. The two youngest children tucked themselves firmly against me in my bed and the other two, who claimed they were way too big to be afraid of a simple storm, nevertheless took comfort from the sound of our nearby voices as we all talked ourselves to sleep.

The well-fed cows were sleeping peacefully in the courtyard when we roused ourselves in the morning and we left them there for Gabriel to take care of when he arrived, full of local news, later in the day. The storm had knocked out electrical wires and telephones throughout the region, a situation that continued for the next six weeks. This created enormous hardships for the entire area—farmers couldn't use their electric milking machines, electric water pumps were non-operational, freezers were out and on and on and on. Actually, as I found out, for the villagers and local farmers, this created a marvelous opportunity to rail against the government. No doubt even the storm was a political conspiracy against their continued comfort. According to local critics, if one of the other parties had been in power, this sort of thing would never have happened.

We, on the other hand, were unaffected. After all, we had neither electricity nor telephone, neither before nor after the storm.

The nightly, climatic temper tantrums continued for the next couple of weeks. We never became quite blasé enough to sleep through them, but we were prepared and thus able to remain comfortably in bed watching the light flashes beyond the closed shutters, shivering at the hurled thunder-claps and finally drifting off to the wash of rainfall on the roof. It was all so elemental. Were the storms a manifestation of my emotions—anger, frustration and despair—at my own solitary condition with a "missing" husband, I wondered, relieving themselves on the world?

Each night, by the time sleep had insinuated itself through the display of cosmic petulance, the two youngest children would position themselves like bookends on either side of me, along with a couple of cats and a dog or two entwined with the assorted limbs. Safety in numbers.

At dawn, *Vezat* floated on a cloud of dense mist rising over the river. The ancient buildings, the fields reaching to the old oak woods which surrounded the property, drifted on an island of fog. The sky above was Wedgewood blue, the sun's rays sparkled on rain-drenched leaves and grass as it poked golden fingers into every saturated corner.

The fog retreated slowly, fighting for every meter as it was pushed back into its river lair. Spires of ancient buildings thrust heavenward. A magic kingdom within the clouds. Rooftop by rooftop, the valley revealed itself: squares of plowed, brown fields, rectangles of soft green foliage and the ribbon of shimmering river curling serenely amongst them, narrow and tree-shaded, then wide and mirrored, absorbing into itself the mist and the magic.

When her kittens were grown, ChiChi, the black and white cat we'd found sitting immobile in the barn, disappeared as quietly as she had arrived. She left her offspring, possibly because the population explosion on the premises was not to her liking. Having been taught to keep their distance, however, the dogs never willingly entered the courtyard until many months after ChiChi's departure.

As the summer green turned to the reds and yellows of fall, Gabriel's thoughts turned to what to do with the cows pastured at *Vezat*. From his point of view, he had three options.

He could move them, but this would require an expenditure of effort on his part and therefore was quite unacceptable.

He could sell them to someone in the area. However, they weren't quite worth the price he intended to ask and everyone hereabouts was fully aware of that fact.

His final and, I'm sure, most promising option was to sell them to *l'Americaine*. Everyone knew that all Americans were rich and what did this one know about the value of heifers anyhow? Contrary to popular opinion, only one of these concepts was true.

One afternoon he arrived at the farm to find me with my hammer attempting to solidify the fence posts around the free-roving beasts. He chuckled over my efforts, even criticizing the placement of the post and my grip on the hammer, while making no attempt to take over the job, then ambled over to the heifers and patted the nearest one affectionately, calling my attention to her sterling qualities. At least, I think that was what he was calling my attention to—my French being rather less extensive than the *agent immobilière's* English when he discussed rooflines or plumbing.

Gabriel spoke very slowly, as to a child, with a great deal of gesturing. The gesturing, I later discovered, was as much a part of the language as the words. Eventually I began to get his message, which was that his cows were INCREDIBLY superb specimens (*les bêtes magnifiques)* and, ESPECIALLY for me (*pour vous, chère madame*), he would sell them at a VERY reduced price (*un prix encroyable*). He would have made a fantastic used car salesman.

I assured him that I would think about it and we spent the next couple of weeks most cordially, with Gabriel at every opportunity pointing out the cows' unsurpassed qualities and his desire to do me the supreme favor of letting me have these magnificent beasts at a price which made them a veritable gift.

During this time, I scoured my English-French dictionary for ways of inquiring about some of the more intimate details about the cows. For instance, I wanted to know if the heifers had been bred and if they were currently with calf. English-French dictionaries, particularly pocket editions, are not terribly informative on livestock terminology. I finally found the word for pregnant—*enceinte*—and tried, slowly and carefully, to work it into the conversation—to absolutely no avail. My pronunciation must have left a lot to be desired and even Gabriel couldn't figure it out. Finally, in desperation, I inquired brightly, "*Sont-elles mariées?*" Are they married?

Gabriel was speechless—for probably the first time in his life. He stared in disbelief, then chuckled...laughed...guffawed and danced around, collapsing in total and absolute hysterics. I looked away in embarrassment...then giggled... then joined in the howling abandon. We shared no common language, our lives had been separated by two continents and our experiences were eons apart, but we were forever bonded by a mutual sense of the ridiculous.

Gabriel never let me forget that incident. I didn't buy his cows, but later I actually sold him a cow or two. Prior to each transaction, he always solemnly inquired, "*Est-ce que elle est mariée?*"

❧ CHAPTER 7 ❧

A Letter Home

Dear Pat,

    You are surely the sister-in-law from heaven! Our heart-felt thanks for the CARE package. I don't understand how French mothers bring up children without peanut butter. The children all seem healthy, and they are amazingly polite, but without peanut butter? Unfathomable. And the tortillas, refried beans and packages of taco and enchilada sauces were inspired. A couple of the kids' new friends stayed for lunch the other day and I fed them tacos and enchiladas. They ate them tentatively at first, then with gusto, and pronounced them *intèressantes*. I took that as a compliment.

    I just know you'd be impressed with my expertise at the local markets. I am. Believe me, it was hard fought. Now I can walk right in to the *boulangerie* and order *un pain et quatre petits pains au chocolat* and actually walk out with what I intended to buy. Although I'm equally certain *la boulangère* is snickering behind her hand over my abominable accent.

All of Europe appears to close up shop during July and August and sort of shuffles its populations, a large percentage of whom inexplicably come to our little spot in the middle of nowhere. *Le Camping* beside the river hosts visitors from Holland, Germany, England and other parts of France and many return every summer. Their attire was rather a shock after seeing my staid neighbors decked out in high necks, long sleeves, cotton stockings and sensible shoes. During July and August, buxom Dutch and Germans along the river sport the teeniest of bikinis and Wendy and Jill giggle hysterically as they tell me that the men look like they're wearing bags of grapes slung from a string across the hips. I'm not sure they need this kind of education.

I can understand why the Dordogne is popular with tourists, it is so stunningly beautiful. The greens are more than just green, the sky a deep indigo blue. And the people are never in a hurry. There's plenty of time for everything and if there isn't, it will just have to be done later. Everything closes down for two hours for lunch, an occasion which is not something to be finished in a hurry. A meal is something to be contemplated, considered and savored. And afterward, digested. And as for shopping on a Sunday, *quelle horreur!*

We visited Lalinde, a village built in the thirteenth century, the other day. Legend has it that in the fourth century A.D., there was a venerated saint, Saint Front, who performed many miracles, mostly improbable, of course. While on a visit to Lalinde, his aid was called on to combat a local nuisance in the form of a dragon who lived in a cave on the far side of the river, and had the unpleasant habit of seizing and eating the boatmen who passed up and down the river by the entrance of his cave. Saint Front sealed the dragon in his lair so that he died and to commemorate this great benefactor, the inhabitants built a church on the hill above the river known as the church of Saint Front de Colaury. The ruins can still be seen from the bridge. I can also verify that we saw boaters on the river, but never caught sight of the dragon, so the legend must be true. There's no dragon there now.

Life, as I knew it, has certainly changed. I've become a wanton woman, at least in the eyes of much of the village. Me, who once walked home from a fraternity party because they served beer and turned the lights off. I guess wantonness is a direct result of not having a husband in residence. Women clutch at their husbands' arms as they pass me on the street. My friend, Gabriel, laughingly told me that everyone assumes he's sleeping with me. When I expressed shock, he assured me that he denies it, of course, but that his stock at *La Taverne* has risen enormously.

And you should see some of these men whose wives are certain I covet. Dentists are apparently not very popular and missing or discolored teeth are common. Bathing isn't all that popular either, but eating most assuredly is. I could tell the good ladies that I'm not lusting in my heart or loins after their prize catches, but that might ruin the fun for everyone.

Oh, my dear, all of us miss all of you so very much. Rob would send his love also if he were here, but he has written that he won't be able to come until around Christmas, when he assures me he'll work on getting us some running water. Hopefully, the electricity will be connected within the next month or two. The French aren't great with time schedules.

The morning hours when I have a moment to write are lovely here. The sun pops over the opposite hill after first announcing its imminent arrival with timid excursions of golden light sparking off the tops of the trees. Then, suddenly it's there, with tiny rainbows flashing from the dew-laden grass.

Much love to all. Please write soon. Thanks again for the package of goodies,

Jan

๑ CHAPTER 8 ๑

Daily Living

Our village of Saint-Cyprien wasn't exactly a metropolis. The business district was about a block long and contained two *quincailleries*, hardware and kitchenware stores. These presented a real problem for me, since the counter was smack at the front of the store and I had to know what I wanted and ask for it. By name. This precluded browsing and required the right name. I did a lot of pointing, ruffling madly through my pocket dictionary. I'm quite sure I gave the *bonnes femmes* at the counter food for conversation and belly laughs.

There were also two *boucheries,* butcher shops. Here again, I was stuck with needing to know what cut of meat to ask for. There was no such thing as prepackaged meats. However, there were a few things under the glass counter to which I could point and hope to get something recognizable.

There must be something in *boucher* school which convinces men that they're irresistible to women, since both of the local butchers were major letches. One was no more than five feet tall and equally wide and had the absolute certainty that he was God's gift to womankind.

"*Bonjour, Madame*. And is your husband in town?"

"*Bonjour, Monsieur.* Oh, I expect him by tomorrow at the latest."

"How lovely you look this morning."

"Yes, it's a beautiful day, *n'est-ce pas*?"

The butcher's wives always seemed to be listening at the door and popped out at the first sound of my voice.

"*Bonjour, Madame.* And how much longer will your vacation be lasting?"

"*Bonjour, Madame.* Ah, yes, the wind is a bit nippy today."

Their chief desire seemed to be to send me on my way and close the door behind me. Someday, I was going to learn how to say "Up yours!" However, we all managed to remain cordial and I usually got some variety of meat and it was up to me to figure out how to cook it.

In the center of town was Chez Borde, where one could purchase plumbing supplies and electrical appliances, large or small, or request plumbing or electrical services. So far, I'd had no such need, having neither electricity nor plumbing. Finally, a benefit of living the "simple life." Next door was a lovely little jewelry shop. I had difficulty believing the farmers gifted their wives with any of the gorgeous but *trés cher* baubles and wondered how the shop remained alive between tourist seasons. I guessed they made do with watch repairs and film developing.

The *librairie* was actually a book store. A library was a *biblioteque* and we didn't have one. One also finds stationery and school supplies in the *librairie*. At some time I'd heard that a good way to learn a language was by actually reading an absorbing book—like a mystery novel—and only stopping to look up a word when one in particular became bothersome. When I discovered a selection of Agatha Christie mysteries in French in paperback editions, I decided to try the method. Some years later, I re-read some of those Christies and was amazed at the differences in the real plot and what my imaginative mind had created. But the method did have some merit in that I acquired the ability to read in French, which differs a great deal from speaking and understanding the language.

Mademoiselle, *la proprietaire* of the *librairie*, was a typical village spinster, hair drawn back in a tight bun and mouth like the straight line on a rag doll. She rarely smiled and the children were terrified of her, but I noticed that she could be quite tender with the shy small ones and made sure they had everything they needed.

Chez Faugère, the *épicerie*, was where I spent the most time—and money. It was the closest thing to a supermarket, only about a tenth the size. Madame Faugère, the proprietor, was tiny, but rocket-fueled. I'd love to eat whatever she ate to give her that kind of energy. She managed her three tall sons, who each had charge of different areas of the store. Marc was the *boucher* and not only didn't he attend the same school as the other *bouchers* in town, he also was kind enough to tell me how to prepare the different meats, just as if I knew enough to ask. Jean-Paul was dark and handsome and newly married and governed the cheese counter, while Eric whipped from stacking shelves to manning the checkout counter. He must have inherited the nuclear reactor inside his mother. They were all charming and treated me like a valued member of the community, without ever prying into my personal life.

One morning, I had laid my purchases on the counter and dug my wallet out of my pocket to discover I was short on cash.

"Oh, dear," I stammered, blushing hotly.

"*Il n'y a pas de problème, Madame.*" Eric laid the ticket in front of me with a pen. "Simply sign the ticket and pay at the end of the month." He said. "Many of our customers do so. *C'est trés commode.*"

I felt welcomed to the community.

Of course, there was also the *patisserie,* with its display of flaky crusted fruit pies, chocolate eclairs stuffed with pure sin and homemade ice cream guaranteed NOT to be missing a single percent butterfat.

I learned to carry my own shopping basket, or better yet, a tiny *ficelle*, a string bag which expanded to hold any number of purchases. I discovered cheeses I'd never heard of and tasted as many as possible. Some were creamy and piquant, some smooth and dotted with herbs, still others reminded me of my sons' gym socks.

Once every month, on a Wednesday, the main street of Saint-Cyprien transformed itself into an open-air market, with stands of merchandise from the large department stores of the country. There were tables spread with housewares of every variety, hardware and the smaller farm implements, household linens, *bleus de travail*—work blues, the uniform of every farmer in the area—shoes and clothes for infants and children, and hanging racks filled with dresses, blouses, sweaters and clothing of all sorts. Hangers in America form a wire shoulder for hanging blouses or sweaters. Hangers in France had additional wire forms which created the shape of a bosom under the garment. And not just any bosom, mind you. This was an excellent example of where the sweater looked a hell of a lot better on the hanger than it ever did on me.

Market fair Wednesday was the one day of the month a person should never try to see the local doctor, for the simple reason that every farmer in the area came into town on that day to shop, to gossip and *boire un coup* with friends. Along with the farmers, every farmer's wife came in to town to tell Dr. DeJean her troubles and to gossip in his waiting room with friends not seen since the prior month.

Our first few months at the farm were rather like a camping vacation, particularly with our lack of running water. We were able to maintain basic cleanliness with water hauled from the spring, but to young Americans born and bred to daily bathing and flushing toilets, it wasn't quite enough.

The Dordogne is a vacation area that draws tourists from all over Europe and we were not immune to its holiday charms. Warm, sunny afternoons found us floating in the river enjoying its cool freshness. The current was just swift enough to give us an invigorating run, taking care not to scrape against the large boulders seemingly slung by the gods into the riverbed. Afterwards we'd drape ourselves on a blanket on the rocky bank to dry ourselves in the sun.

At least once a week, we grabbed bars of soap and shampoo and headed to Belvès, a neighboring village with a public swimming pool. The pool was fun, but what we really went for were the showers in the dressing rooms. The boys took their bars of soap and shampoo and the girls and I took ours and positively luxuriated. What heaven to stand under a stream of *warm* water, scrubbing skin and hair. I doubt that any of us had ever treasured the feel of cleanliness to such an extent. We also made sure to utilize the toilet facilities while we were there. I will always believe that the public swimming pool in Belvès was what saved me from a permanent state of constipation. Did you ever try to relax and concentrate while seated on a metal bucket in the open air?

We suffered a major loss when the pool closed at the start of the school year.

When we had a few spare hours, the kids and I would climb into the car and investigate the valley. We visited the *Chateau de Beynac*, which stands at the top of an almost vertical cliff rising from the banks of the Dordogne. The castle was the site of many battles and has been built and rebuilt on several occasions. The old fortress was the seat of one of the four baronnies in Périgord and includes a double ring of outer walls overlooking the plateau, while on the south side the cliff face itself constitutes an impregnable system of defense.

The vast rooms have been carefully restored, containing stone-mullioned windows and great bays, and a huge quadrangular keep with an adjacent staircase tower. This keep extends into the main apartments with a machicolated parapet walkway that overlooks a triangular building dating from the fourteenth century. The Chamber of States has ribbed barrel vaulting and was used by the States of Périgord whose members represented all the region's nobility. The private chapel next to the Chamber has frescoes dating from the fifteenth century.

We found an excellent example of early plumbing adjacent to one of the large upper rooms in a small circular extension containing a stone seat with a central hole opening onto a rose garden about fifty feet below. I'll bet those roses were magnificent.

We also visited the village of La Roque-Gageac, strung out between cliffs and the river in a setting so outstanding it has earned the picturesque place the title of "the most beautiful village in France." Protected by its walls, La Roque never fell into English hands during the One Hundred Years' War nor into Protestant hands during the Wars of Religion. Yet what time or warfare had not succeeded in destroying was very suddenly wiped out by nature on January 17, 1957 at 10:30 in the morning when a gigantic piece of rock detached itself from the cliff face and crashed down, demolishing houses and causing a number of deaths. The village has since been restored and the sixteenth century church still perches on the cliff above.

The children especially liked the chateau at Les Milandes, which was first built in the fifteenth century and underwent extensive alterations in the last century. It is best known as the home made by the jazz singer, Josephine Baker, for her adopted children from all over the world, forming a sort of international village. By the time of our stay, the chateau was open to the public for viewing, both the interiors and the extensive grounds.

On these outings, we loved to sit alongside the river and have a picnic lunch, discussing what we had seen that morning. It certainly changes one's perspective to see evidence of civilizations long past and of lives, once vibrant and active, now consigned to history books. We were also constantly amazed at what tremendous architectural feats had been accomplished without the use of modern equipment and machinery.

Of course, my brood liked plentiful free time to simply play or be with friends. The local kids were a friendly lot and the farm rapidly took on the same clamorous aspects as our backyard in New Jersey. Pierre and Hèléne lived at the foot of the hill, children of the local mason. Hèléne was Wendy's age and Pierre a couple of years older, having reached the desirable age at which he was allowed moped privileges. Dominique, Gabriel's nephew, was an age somewhere between Wendy and Danny and had all the makings of a young delinquent.

Danny immediately brought out the bats, balls and gloves and started instruction in the gentle art of baseball. Pierre brought a soccer ball. The baseballs eventually all wound up irretrievably lost in the woods and soccer became the game-of-the-month.

"You can hit the ball with your *head*, Mom!"

"Can we get our own ball, so we can practice?"

One afternoon, Dominique and a couple of boys I hadn't seen before decided to ride the calves. Tim came to find me.

"Mom, I think you better come see," he said.

One boy was astraddle a calf, another had a rope around her neck pulling and the third was behind pushing. I was furious.

"Tim, make them stop."

"I can't, Mom. I tried."

I tried to pull out something in my limited French.

"*Lechez-les! Lechez-les!*" I called.

The boys stopped instantly, released the calf and stared at me before breaking into hysterical laughter. My own kids were giggling quietly.

"What'd I say?" I asked warily.

Tim was nothing, if not tactful. "I think you meant *laissez-les*, Mom. That means 'let them go.' You actually told them to 'lick' the calves."

"Good try, Mom," said Dan with a grin.

"Well, it worked," I said, going back in the house.

French 101

It was now September on the farm. The summer had fled, fall taking its place. The night air descended, soft and densely black. I couldn't recall ever knowing such darkness, which penetrated the senses first by sound, rustling, padding. My eyes, light-filled, adjusted, accepting shadow images cast by the waning moon.

Fall is an enchanting season. The air becomes crisper, skies clearer. Perhaps knowing that leaves, flowers and birds will soon depart makes their presence more desirable, giving a feel of bittersweet nostalgia. In the southwest of France, the air takes on a golden quality, tinting the river and haloing each tree and blade of grass. Now, with the first stirrings of autumn, the children were scheduled to start school. It inspired in me the desire to learn as well. It was time, I decided in a rush of enthusiasm, to master French.

Learning a new language is like passing through a black hole and coming out the other side, thought processes transformed, emotional centers shifted and rationality suspended. Food and shelter are basic necessities of life. Communication is a requirement for obtaining these and is, thus, an even greater need. Perhaps even more important is the fact that humans are very social beings. Few can survive isolation.

We've established the principle. It was only left to implement it.

I brought my children to the village school where they were distributed into the appropriate classes based upon their ages. Their faces expressed varying degrees of bewilderment, incomprehension and sheer terror as they were borne off, one by one, by groups of chattering children of similar shapes and sizes, but speaking in unknown tongues. I smiled encouragement with tears pooling behind my eyes, feeling like Quisling in the act of betraying his people.

I threw myself into barn cleaning with a savage ferocity, clutching the pitchfork and tossing ancient cow turds with abandon. Grueling work was little enough punishment for a mother who would abandon her own children. I pictured them terrified, bravely holding back tears in front of jeering foreigners, each one suffering alone, away from the comfort of the others. I tried to blame their heartless father who had sent us away into this exile. That didn't work. I was their mother. It was up to me to provide their first line of defense and I had failed them.

That first day I stood in front of the school waiting half an hour before the final bell rang, thoroughly expecting soul-battered children to limp out the doors and run sobbing to my arms. I did not anticipate the laughing young persons who emerged loaded with books, calling back, *"Ciao,"* "Bye," *"Adieu," "Salut."*

"Hey, mom, I can say all the body parts. Even those... well...you know." Danny snickered suggestively.

"And I can say pee and poop in French," chimed in Tim, giggling.

"Mom, I have a new friend. Her name is Nicole," little Jill whispered to me while her brothers compared notes raucously in the back of the van.

"Mother, you just won't believe—boys, will you be quiet!—you simply won't believe it! Mom, make them stop!" Wendy required total attention for her statements.

"My English teacher—her accent is terrible!—she said I don't speak English, I speak American. Just because I corrected her grammar. And it's the same, Mother, isn't it? I was right, I know I was."

I drew in my first clear breath of the day. They had survived! It was going to be all right.

I don't understand how children can learn a language so quickly. They have a remarkable facility for curling their tongues around their palates to create new and unique sounds as well as curling their minds around new and unique ways of expressing their thoughts. It's like a process of osmosis. In two months, they understood everything said to them in French, in six months they were fluent.

My mental processes were less fluid. Of course, I wasn't in school eight hours a day. My only conversations were with the butcher, the baker, the grocer and Gabriel. With the butcher, the baker and the grocer, I did a lot of pointing and I was learning the monetary system. Dividing by five to give me the American equivalent was easy.

Soon after we arrived, I had quickly discovered that milk wasn't sold in the village stores and finally figured out that was because we lived in an area where three out of four farmers had milk cows. Similar to stocking coal in a market in Newcastle, oil at the pharmacy in Saudi Arabia or ice cubes in Alaska. I was sent to the hardware store to purchase a milk *bidon,* a two-litre replica of the farmers' thirty-litre containers. Then I was directed to a neighbor up the hill who had a farm. At the hour of milking, I was told, I could buy milk fresh from the cow.

I took Tim with me to act as interpreter as I headed to the Rougier farm the next evening at 6:00 P.M. We followed the sounds of cattle munching and rattling their chain collars into a huge barn. Monsieur Rougier had a large herd, about thirty cows, in an immaculate barn. Each cow was ensconced in fresh straw laid out on a cement floor. There were drains spaced at intervals and I could see that the floor was hosed down regularly. It looked freshly scrubbed. The cows were happily eating hay out of raised mangers and scarcely bothered to look around at the strangers entering their dining hall.

The milking equipment was equally modern with tubes running the length of the ceiling carrying the milk to a large refrigerated unit. Milking hoses descended to milk four cows simultaneously. M. and Mme. Rougier watched these hoses carefully, but Madame moved over to welcome us.

"Bonjour, Madame. Bonjour, jeune homme."

"Bonjour, Madame. Du lait, s'il vous plaît." How about that? I actually asked for some milk. *Hey, this is easy*, I thought, mentally patting myself on the back.

"Bien sûr. Un moment."

And then everything sort of went to pieces. M'sieur Rougier walked over, shook hands and asked me something, heaven only knows what. I sure didn't. Neither did Tim.

Eventually, even after slowing down and smiling a lot, we all shrugged—very French, the shrug—and shook hands one more time. They filled my *bidon*, I held out a hand with several coins in it, they took a couple and we all smiled again as Tim and I departed.

This went on every night for the next year. I now knew exactly how much money I needed, but was no closer to conversing. I did discover, much to my amazement, that I understood more and more of what they said to me. And was appalled. They asked questions which, in my naivete, I would never dream of asking total strangers. How much did we pay for *Vezat?* Why wasn't my husband with us? Where was he? How much money did he send us? How long were we going to stay? And as my comprehension grew, I became more cunning. Of course, they didn't realize that I was beginning to understand nuances and meanings. Our conversations became widely divergent as I fielded their probing.

"Combien est-ce que vous avez payez pour Vezat?" How much did you pay for the farm?

"Oh oui, c'est très beau." Yes, it's very lovely.

"Et votre mari? Il revien bientôt?" This from Madame. She was most interested in my marital status, never for an instant leaving me alone with her husband.

"Oui." Sure. He'll be back next blue moon, I thought, my bitterness surfacing.

"Il vous envoie l'argent?" Always that money question.

"Oh, oui. Il va bien." His health is great.

As time passed and my fluency in the language increased, their questions became more pointed and insistent. Fortunately, by that time I had my own milk cows.

We began speaking French at home. This was at my request so that the children could help me with my faltering verbs. *En famille,* we tended to mix both languages, starting out at a 20/80 (French/English) mix and, over time, reversing the percentages to 80/20, creating a bastardized language only we could understand. It was fun, of course, and made us feel terribly international and intellectual. We made random selections of the best word in each language for what we were trying to express, as in "Let's go to the *cinema* this evening. It's a *très amusante* film."

In the beginning, we spoke our unique form of *franglais* only among ourselves, but habits are insidious. They tend to pop up all by themselves and when we started noticing a friend or neighbor looking puzzled at something we'd said and ran it back through our minds, we realized what we were doing. It was like a cat speaking with a dog and mixing the meows up with the woofs.

I discovered another interesting aspect of familiarity with a new language, the lack of emotional pull of certain words. For instance, I was raised in a household where my mother allowed no swearing by my dad or brother if I were within earshot. This produced a grown woman in whom a simple "Damn" raised the hairs on the back of my neck and caused a deep blush on my face. To my surprise, words far down on the obscenity scale in French produced no *frisson* at all. As the months of listening to Gabriel's rakish renditions of the language passed, I could have conversed with a group of marines. My kids, shocked, nipped this in the bud.

On the other hand, being completely fair and non-partisan, in a comparison of French and English blue language, the French win hands down. Americans tend to stick to one or two English curse words repeated ad nauseum. A really cranky Frenchman can swear creatively for half an hour, discussing your antecedents and other barnyard relatives along with their many and varied sexual practices, and never duplicate a single word.

✎ CHAPTER 10 ✎

The Indispensable Tool

As I became acquainted with the villagers, I noticed every *paysan* owned a pocket knife. No farmer would be without that useful, nay obligatory, tool for cutting the twine on a bale of hay, for scraping a battery connection clean of accumulated grease and goop or for cutting his *biftek* at dinner. He would have felt naked in the wind without it. The little tool seemed to be more essential to him than the fingers on his hand and, in fact, he could actually do quite well and often did, without all of the prescribed ten digits. It is not uncommon when shaking hands with a neighbor or visitor, I discovered, that one or two of the fingers on his hand are mere stumps. Involuntarily, I would glance at the hand and the man, lifting it to his face, would look surprised to note that it wasn't complete, then he would shrug and grin and announce that the appendages were lost to the *engreneur* while removing the grains of corn from the cob or to the *faucheuse*, the hay cutter, while testing its operation or to one of the many sharp-toothed implements of farming which require a keen eye and quick reflexes. Then he would proceed to tell the story of M'sieur Hublot across the hill who lost his entire right hand when the tractor hitch gave out while he was sharpening his plow. *Eh oui. Pauvre vieux!*

I spent several weeks utilizing the larger tools of my new trade, a pitchfork and shovel and carrying a small battery of pliers, wire cutters and scythe around the fence line. In the absence of the all-purpose pocket knife, I placed a small paring knife in the barn for cutting open bales. Seeking me out in the barn one afternoon, Gabriel announced that we were invited to his home for dinner and to meet his wife.

"Rien d'especial. Un petit repas."

Nothing special, indeed! We knew by now that a *little* meal in the Dordogne didn't exist. The region was famous for its *foie gras* and other goose products, especially its *confits* and *pâtés*, as well as rustic stews, earthy black truffles and meaty field mushrooms, such as *champignons des près*, a white button mushroom with a light mauve coating under the cap, the orange-hued *catalanes* and *verdanes*, a pungent, silvery purple specimen. The wines of the region were superb and *eau de noix*, a walnut liqueur, divine.

At Chez Faugère I carefully selected a bottle of wine, *un vin vieux,* to take to our host and, at the stated hour, we presented ourselves at his home. The living quarters were reached by climbing a set of outside stairs to the second level. The all-purpose room contained the usual enormous fireplace with a small black and white cat curled into a cupped andiron, a sink with a pump handle on one side, a wood stove and a small work table on the other and a long wooden table which stretched from one side of the room to the other.

Thick, white crockery dishes lined the table in front of long, wooden benches.

Madame was pretty and plump, like a ripe pear turned upside down. She was as shy and quiet as Gabriel was outgoing. As the evening progressed, she surprised us with an occasional bit of dry, caustic wit, but her main contribution was an outstanding meal of gourmet quality.

We started off with large bowls of a creamy *soupe aux poireaux*, a variety of onion, steamy and delicious. Following the soup, a large platter was passed filled with thinly sliced potatoes, beets and hard-boiled eggs in a *sauce vinaigrette*. Gabriel passed the loaf of bread whole, but, seeing me hesitate then start to break off a morsel, he quickly whipped out his handy universal knife and sliced off generous chunks for each of us. I'd seen him use that same knife to cut the twine on a bale of hay and to scrape grease off a tractor part. I called a quick halt to other distasteful mental pictures.

The next course was an aromatic platter of *coq au vin*, a chicken cooked in wine with bacon bits adding their own special flavorings.

"Napoleon was a great old cock, but the young 'uns were starting to give him a licking," Gabriel grinned and raised his glass in toast to the old rooster. "I bet it took half the day to tenderize the old rascal."

I quickly set down my fork and sipped at the wine. I truly disliked eating meat which had a name and a personality.

"My, that was a wonderful meal," I murmured, wiping my lips.

"Nonsense! Why, we've barely started. *Mangez! Mangez!*"

Gabriel was ever the genial host, a purveyor of wines and a raconteur. He had a special wine for each course, exhorting me as each dish was replaced with another, to drink up, another vintage must be tasted. If I hadn't been watchful, the children's glasses would have been filled as well.

"Buvez! Buvez! Il y en a encore!"

I soon learned he wasn't kidding about being barely started and I made a mental note to pace myself better the next time I dined *chez* Gabriel. The chicken was followed by *rosbif au jus*, sliced thin and pink, fork tender and succulent, served with baby new potatoes in melted butter and fresh asparagus. I was in serious gastric pain by now, but couldn't bear to see the look of distress cross Madame's face at the thought that I didn't like her beautifully prepared meal. I looked over and saw even the children were slowing down, though I'd always thought they were bottomless pits.

Following the roast came a crisp, fresh salad. The theory behind the salad at the end of the meal is that it refreshes the palate before a sweet. And sure enough, we were then served a home-baked *tarte aux pêches* followed by a platter of several different cheeses. At the salad, Gabriel changed the red wine to a light, sweeter white. It was tough to find room for even one more sip.

Gabriel saw me struggling. "You Americans don't eat enough to keep a bird alive. How do you expect to keep up your strength?" he said, shaking his head.

Though Gabriel started the evening serious and sober in his status of host and man of the household, as the food and wine took hold, he became the same teasing jokester I had come to know and grow fond of. He bantered with the boys, teased the girls and me and asked many questions about America. I noticed that both Gabriel and his wife treated the children as if they were adults.

"Mademoiselle Wendy, did you ride horses in America?"

"Oh yes, I had my own horse in America, too. Her name was Candy." Wendy looked wistful.

"And did you ride her to school?"

"No. We took the bus."

I mentioned that we had family living in Arizona and Gabriel asked, "Do they carry guns all the time?"

"For heaven's sakes, why?" I asked.

"In case they see Indians, of course."

"Oh, Gabriel, it's not like that any more."

Our movie and television industry have a lot to answer for, I thought.

After dinner, I offered to help clean up but was waved off indignantly. "You are guests!" Gabriel insisted.

As we prepared to leave, I glanced at the sink in the corner of the kitchen with its pump handle instead of a faucet and felt fleeting nostalgia for the days when we took things like faucets and in-door plumbing for granted.

"*Merci*," I said at the door. "*C'etait delicieux*." Outside, I could barely waddle to the car. On the way back up the hill, I vowed that I would stop the very next day at the *quincaillerie* and acquire my own pocketknife. Without the proper tools, how could I ever become a *paysan?*

My wine-soaked brain forgot, of course, but while I was muddling around in the barn later that week, I cleaned some old moldy hay off the ancient rabbit hutches and there, slightly rusted but fully operational, lay THE TOOL! A pocket knife. Reverently, I took it to the kitchen and, with a rag and some oil, cleaned it. The knife was very basic, one blade which folded into a carved handle. It was no bigger than the palm of my hand. Perfect.

With pride, I stuffed it into my pocket and expected to lose it within the week. I habitually lose everything which is not attached to me by flesh. But the knife, which had appeared so magically, remained in my possession by the same means. Oh yes, I lost it with regularity. But it always managed to turn up again; falling out of a bale of hay, appearing in a crevice of the tractor, popping out of a pile of dirty laundry.

As I grew more and more accustomed to myself in my new role of female farmer, I wondered if I would ever again eat in a fine restaurant and, if I did, whether I would automatically whip out my trusty blade to cut my bread or meat. And what would be the reaction of a sophisticated waiter?

७० CHAPTER 11 ॐ

Home Improvements

The children and I wrote weekly letters to Rob detailing our progress and activities. Rob wrote back, perhaps a bit less often and his letters were considerably shorter, but then, I told myself, he was very busy.

I made a determined effort to keep my epistles light-hearted and positive, recounting what fun it was to bathe in the river and visit the public swimming pool in a neighboring village once or twice a week with shampoo in hand. Unfortunately, the pool closed in the fall and then we shampooed in the "brain freezer," which was Wendy's name for the water coming out of the short hose draped in the spring which required heavy-duty sucking to prime it before water flowed. We all wondered at Wendy's rare good-heartedness which prompted her to set the example and go first, until we realized the water left in the hose had warmed in the sun. After that, when hair washing was necessary, it was a race to be first.

Blithely, I told Rob how everyone took turns carrying buckets up to the house from the spring, without mentioning the bitching that took place every step of the way. Wendy and the boys struggled up the hill with two buckets each trip and even little Jill managed a small, two-handed bucket. Unfortunately, most of the water sloshed out on the way to the kitchen.

In my letters, I described in excruciating detail my linguistic attempts to deal with the bureaucracy of the electric company as I tried to get a line to the house—and their nonchalant disregard for the passage of time.

"Bien, bien, Madame, bientôt...a toute a l'heure...la semaine prochaine...ou le mois après...ne vous inquietez pas." Soon—next week—next month—don't worry. The attitude became contagious. After all, what did it really matter whether we had electricity to the house? There weren't any wires inside the house anyway.

I compared my dealings with the French officials to trying to catch a Slinky in mid-slink or pushing against a ball of Play-Doh. You push in at one spot, it bubbles out at another. Always polite...suave...understanding...immovable.

Rob's next visit was slated for Christmastime. The time passed more quickly than I thought. Soon December arrived, with days that were glorious, crisp and bright and every night saw a sprinkling of frost like sequins scattered over the meadow. We picked him up at the Bordeaux airport, a three-hour drive away and excitement bubbled out of everyone at once.

Danny was especially excited. "Dad, I'm learning to play soccer. It's really neat. You use your head like a bat!" Since most of Danny's baseballs had been forever lost in the woods surrounding the pastures, a new love was taking its place.

Jill echoed her brother's bright mood. "Daddy, can I show you the baby bunnies? They're just barely out of their nest and they're so cute. And we might have some baby chickens soon. I help Mommy lots." Jill was enchanted with the burgeoning animal population.

Wendy was more contained. "Can we get my horse while you're here? You promised." Wendy hadn't forgotten the promise given so easily. She was calling him on his pledge.

Rob looked to me for help. I gazed out the car window and said nothing.

The next day we visited a nearby dealer in livestock. Slender and dapper, dark hair slicked back tight against his head, he moved and spoke in quick, nervous bursts. He brought to mind an image of a racetrack tout. Of course, all I had were mental images, having never personally seen one. But, believe me, he fit the picture.

He also had some very pretty horses. Wendy cast her eyes on a three-year-old black filly with a white star and two white socks, gentle eyes and a mischievous lilt to her head and fell in love. Add to this the challenge that the filly was barely trained and the sale was made.

Unfortunately for Rob, I also fell in equine love and decided to cash in on his promise to me of long-standing. The object of my passion was a huge grey, a hunter with thoroughbred lines and soft dark eyes. We stood at one side of the pasture, he nuzzling my arm, me caressing his neck and ears. We mutually declared our devotion. I pleaded, the dapper man saw dollar signs and made a one-time-only offer which was further sweetened by the addition of a pair of adorable baby calves. A decision was made and Rob's guilty conscience paid the bill.

By the time we left, we had only to wait for delivery of two horses and two three-month old calves. We walked off with visions of "gentleman farming" or perhaps I should say "lady farming," a restored ranch house with dark woods gleaming against heavy stone, pastures surrounded by white rail fences filled with glossy horses and chubby cattle, riding wooded trails while faithful family retainers maintained clean, sweet-smelling stables and polished the furniture. Oh my God! Talk about delusional.

We proudly showed Rob the clean barns, over which we had scattered a bedding of hay found in the big hay barn. These would be perfect for our new additions as soon as they arrived. We decided there was probably enough of the old hay for feed until the spring haying and Rob went shopping for a used tractor. I was beginning to feel like a real farmer.

We bought a new fence battery and started work on the fence line. We'd need at least one of the pastures right away to provide grazing for our new acquisitions. Working together while the kids were in school gave us time to talk, time we hadn't had much of in the last year.

"Rob, I've been thinking, what will you do when you're over here full time? I mean, besides farming."

He seemed ill-at-ease and stammered, "Well, you know, the printing company is a long way from showing enough profit to sell. And the market is way too unstable and depressed to risk a public offering. I'll have lots of time to think of something."

"But you don't even speak the language. Do you think we made this move a little hastily?" I challenged.

"Of course not! And it's wonderful for the kids. They seem to be settling into school really well."

I studied his face, unvoiced questions crowding my mind. "They are," I said quietly. "But they need a father. And I miss you."

"Don't worry. It won't be long. And I'll be here so often you won't have a chance to miss me. C'mon, let's go over and I'll show you how to drive the tractor."

The subject was changed, but nothing was resolved. I realized my question hadn't even been answered. A niggle of worry settled into my heart and mind.

We spent a lot of time making sketches of the building and marking out a kitchen, living area, bedrooms and baths and indulging in huge amounts of dreaming. Our evenings were spent playing cards and board games under our hanging kerosene lantern with a roaring fire in the huge fireplace.

A few days before Christmas, the boys and their dad went out and cut a pine tree which we all decorated together. The skies were sunny and bright, we sang carols, we went through all the rituals of gift buying, wrapping presents behind closed doors in great secrecy so we could indulge in an orgy of gift opening on Christmas morning.

The horses and calves were delivered the next day and the property began to take on the look of a real farm. The overturned bucket in the outhouse required exposing bare body parts to icy metal, however, and Rob suddenly decided we needed indoor plumbing.

"A little elbow grease, that's all it takes, a little elbow grease. We don't need to hire out work we can just as well do ourselves."

It turned out we did have to hire someone to put in the monster septic tank, but we all took turns digging the enormous pit for it during the Christmas vacation. In all honesty, I must admit that Rob did a yeoman's job. I guess the children's butts and mine had partially toughened up to that frigid metal bucket but we were happy to say good-bye to the outhouse, visions of indoor flushable potties dancing in our heads.

Buying pipes and tubing created its own challenges. An American businessman, like Rob, working against short time-lines, develops some frustration when dealing with the local suppliers.

"Eh bien, oui, peut-être la semaine prochaine. C'est Noël, vous savez." But Rob wasn't about to accept a delivery next week...maybe, Christmas or not, and took himself off to the next larger town and then the next, picking up the supplies himself. Shortly after Christmas, most of the trenching was dug, about half the pipe was laid and the septic tank was scheduled for delivery...perhaps...by mid-January. But Rob said he had important commitments in Washington before the end of the year. Besides, snow flurries were threatening and he was catching a cold, so he bid us goodbye and flew back to the States.

For the next few days, a chilly sun sparked incandescently off the glistening snow covering the holes and ditches. Then it warmed, just enough to create seas of mud throughout the courtyard. The horses risked their slender limbs every time we moved them in or out of the stables with the open ditch directly in front buried in the muck. We laid plank walkways which disappeared daily, absorbed by some wicked mud troll.

A crew arrived to scope out the spot for the septic tank and shook their heads sadly.

"C'est pas possible." (Not possible.)

"Le boue est trop epais." (Too much mud.)

"Vaut mieux foutre la fosse la-bas?" (That's not the right place for a septic tank, how about over there?)

"Mon dieu, quelle merde!" (My God, what *&^%$#@!)

They drove away. I cried.

In late May, after many negotiations that involved reasoning, begging and weeping, the men and the septic tank returned, the crew selected the location, dug the hole and left the tank in place. Not connected to any pipes, of course, and totally uncovered, but there. Shortly thereafter, Rob returned, re-dug the trenches after removing the planks which had been sucked down through the mud and hooked up a couple miles of pipes. On this visit, he stayed long enough to complete the sewage system, install a water pump and tank under the shelter of the patriarchal oak beside the spring and hook up the electrical system to the meter which a sad-eyed utility man had finally connected, after removing a dead mouse and a family of spiders.

Luxury is relative. Some require heated towel racks, a tubside holder for champagne glasses, Jacuzzi tubs, marble countertops. For us, making our home in a foreign land on a primitive farm, it was a flushable toilet on a stone floor surrounded by roof and walls, which didn't quite meet. It was a sink with water which ran both hot and cold and a shower stall with the same features. This was living.

The room selected for these marvels of modern technology was an ancient pig stall at the opposite end of the house/barn structure from the sleeping quarters. Next to the pig barn were two old stables which we had decided were the perfect spot for a new kitchen, located, as it was, right next to the water lines.

All this was part of our master plan which would eventually turn the long, rambling structure in which we lived into a long, rambling farmhouse, utilizing the heavy oak beams and massive stones and adding large glass windows and flooring. I also harbored covetous, longing thoughts about heating and insulation. The livestock would need to make other living arrangements, but that was a bridge to cross later. Much later. Perhaps never.

Rob visited twice that year and each stay lasted two weeks. On his next sojourn, we again eagerly drove the three hours to Bordeaux, the nearest international airport, greeted him with kisses and hugs and everyone talked non-stop and simultaneously the entire trip home. We discussed the current home improvement project for the visit in great detail and outlined each job. He was a bit vague about how much longer it would take to sell the printing company and about his eventual plans for joining us.

"These things take time, you know. Besides the time just isn't right for a sale. The company isn't doing too well. Did you get the tiles for the kitchen floor? Oh for God's sake, what's the holdup this time?"

The first week he suffered from jet lag, business stress and stomach problems from the change in diet. The following week we began bickering about the local tradespeople, discussing why it was my own fault I couldn't prime the water pump and the kids went back to conversing at the dinner table in French, telling their father that if he stuck around longer he might learn the language.

"After all, Dad, isn't that why we're here?"

I hated to admit it, but it was almost a relief to wave him off at the airport.

"You know, I really enjoy taking you to Bordeaux to catch the plane for the States." I was putting the finishing touches on his suitcase.

"You like seeing me leave again? You got something going around here?" He didn't know whether I was kidding or not.

"No, of course not. It's just that..." I wasn't sure how he'd take this either, "It's just that, well, it's the only time I ever get a kiss from you anymore." I kept my eyes directed on the contents of the suitcase. No accusations. The last thing I wanted was a confrontation. Bringing up the subject that had begun to nip at my thoughts might make it real.

Silence. Then he blustered. "Oh, for Pete's sake, that's just not true. Besides, I've been working so hard and I didn't feel at all well, and...you know."

Where had it gone? The special quality Rob and I had right from the start of our relationship. Of being two halves of one whole. Trite, but it seemed to fit. At least, I thought it did. Then again, I told myself, it was probably the separation, the worries, the children. Everything would be great just as soon as we all were together here on the farm.

The kids chattered most of the way to Bordeaux.

"Why don't you get the mason down the hill, what's his name? You know who I mean. Anyway, see what he'd charge to do the kitchen. Just the floor, the windows and doors and install the cabinets we picked out. If he's not too expensive, you can go ahead. Might be awhile before I get back."

"M'sieur Delpit? You mean it? Oh, that's great! I'll ask him right away."

Arriving at our destination, we hugged and kissed long and lovingly. Saying goodbye at airports had become the highlight of my love life. But this time I was able to see Rob off without tears.

A kitchen. We were going to have a real kitchen!

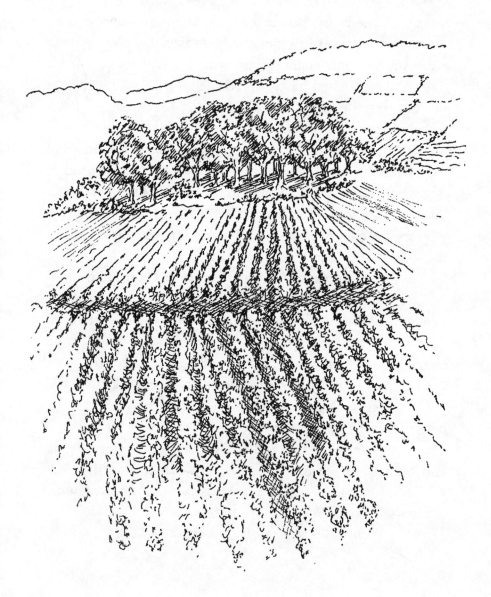

❧ CHAPTER 12 ❧

Special Wine

Since the eleventh century wine has been produced commercially in the Dordogne, particularly in the Bergerac area, in which mostly *Cabernet Sauvignon, Cabernet Franc* and *Malbec* grapes produce the red wines and *Sémillon, Sauvignon* and *Muscadelle* grapes are grown for the white. While there are over ninety commercial vineyards in the region, there exist untold numbers of small, private vineyards on farms. As I grew to know the countryside, I became convinced that nine out of every ten farms in the area bounded roughly on the north by the English Channel, the south by the Mediterranean, and on either side by Spain and Switzerland—otherwise known as *La Belle France*—had a couple of acres devoted to its personal vineyard. If anything, that number is probably low. Certainly, in our region, the Dordogne, every farmer made his own wine. And the farms were known by their particular wines.

Grapevines thrive in rocky soil, thrusting their roots deep in every crook and crevice. Tending the vines is a year-long process of cutting and trimming and tying the branches to horizontal wires, of weeding between the rows and fertil-izing, of a constant war waged against weevils, bugs, snails and miscellaneous critters who love the tender green shoots and mildew, a terrible blight countered by rising before the morning dew to dust the leaves with a special powder.

The timing of the *vendange*, the grape harvest, is highly personal. The farmer tests the weather, checks the Almanac, the phase of the moon, the direction of the wind and, with infinite care, surveys the clusters of vivid purple and rosy grapes. Then he announces the day and spreads the word to friends and neighbors.

A *vendange* must be completed in one day. None of this dribbling grapes into a *cuve* little by little. The fermenta-tion process must start all at one time. Therefore, as many people as possible are gathered, both children and adults, given baskets and pruning shears and sent off down the rows, snipping the wiry stems and placing the grape bunches in the baskets. As a basket is filled, it is emptied onto the *remorque* to be refilled again. And again. And again. It's fun. A happy time of neighborly gossip, teasing and laughter.

Finally, a tractor pulls the *remorque* as close as possi-ble to the *cuve*, which is usually located in the corner of a barn. A *cuve* is a big oaken barrel. I mean BIG. Ours was about seven feet high and even bigger around. It was located in a back corner of the hay barn and, since the hay stuffed every corner of the barn, we had to leave a narrow pathway from a side door to provide access.

The bunches of grapes are run through a manual clothes wringer to extract most of the juice—no, we didn't mash them with our bare feet—then juice and pulp are dumped together into the *cuve*. The children are thoroughly purpled, head to foot, and the adults aren't much better. At this point, all the helper families retire to their own homes to clean up and tend to evening milking and chores. After which the entire group reconvenes at the host farm for feasting and much tasting and discussion of last year's wine, politics and gossip.

The wine from each farm has its own distinct taste from the blend of grape varieties and from the state of ripeness when picked. One of our neighbors up the hill, M'sieur Tabanou, was reputed always to pick his grapes too green, producing a decidedly acidic wine. Gabriel's comments on his neighbors' efforts were pungent and to the point.

"Son vin est trop vert." His wine is too green.

"Son vin est trop mûr." His wine is too ripe.

"Le pauvre con fait jamais du bon vin." The poor jerk never makes a good wine.

Once the juiced grapes are deposited in the *cuve,* one must allow time for the mixture to rest and ferment. In my venture into wine making, I peered into the bubbling mess daily, watching and listening to it gurgle, and felt like one of Hamlet's witches. When the activity slows and ceases, in ten days to two weeks, the juice is poured off through a wooden spigot at the base of the *cuve*, filtered scientifically through a clump of straw. Gabriel joined me to taste the year's bounty and pronounce its readiness. Any opportunity for a glass of wine was good.

I poured some into bottles and tightly corked them. The rest I placed in oak barrels and stored them in a cool, dark corner of the barn to meditate and gain wisdom as the wine aged. As each barrel is tapped, the rest of the wine needs to be bottled immediately. Any air inside turns the balance into vinegar.

New wine has a bite on the tongue, a nip to the palate, like an unbroken colt kicking its heels at the sky. But the flavor, oh, yes, the flavor, of crisp chill nights and somnolent sunny days, full of fruit, spice, rain, frost and a hint, a mere *soupçon,* of oak.

Once the wine is drained from the *cuve,* many of my neighbors pour sugar over the remaining grape skins which pulls out even more of the juices and starts a second fermentation. The result is a *vin cuite*, which is commonly served as an *aperitif.*

Now it was time for cleanup. The dried grape carcasses all had to be hauled out of the *cuve* and deposited elsewhere. Considering them organic vegetation, I decided to fling them onto the field in front of the barn as mulch. The process should have been simple, but I hadn't taken into account the alcohol content which remained. After descending into the *cuve,* scooping a couple of buckets, climbing out and tossing the contents onto the field three or four times, I was falling-down drunk and had a raging headache. I tried holding my breath and wound up flat on my face in the middle of the mush. Eventually, I completed the job over the period of a week but swore off wine for at least a month.

On the other hand, the chickens found the grape peels to be a marvelous addition to their diet. They wound up weaving around the fields, clucking riotously and depositing eggs wherever and whenever.

When we first arrived, Gabriel mourned the vineyard at *Vezat,* which had a reputation as one of the best in the area. It had been planted before World War II and was a mature *vigne* with an excellent mix of plants. Unfortunately, my knowledge of caring for a *vigne* was about equal to my knowledge of quantum physics. In the interests of the vineyard, however, and his continuing access to its final product, Gabriel became our instructor in the fine art of wine making.

We had lots of lessons to learn on all aspects of farming. Though I was a sucker for anything on four legs, the closest I'd ever been to an actual working farm was from the road in passing. And while for many of the farming processes we had been granted the most *insouciant* teacher in all of France, possibly in the entire Western World, for wine making and care of a *vigne,* we had a Grand Master. When the heart is involved in the work, can excellence be far behind?

Thumper

We lived for a year *sans* electricity for the most part, so television was an academic issue. We spent our evenings playing every board game known to man or child: Monopoly, Candyland, Scrabble. We tried to use our increasing horde of French words in the Scrabble games. The kids always beat me hands-down.

French television in our village wasn't a twenty-four hour a day thing. There was news and for the lunch break a variety show from 11:30 A.M. until 1:00 P.M., then programming started again at five in the afternoon until ten or eleven at night. There was agitation amongst the elderly and bedridden for daylong programming, but the general consensus was that enough was enough. I was inclined to agree.

Once we acquired electricity, we had a choice between two channels, but one was generally political debates and academic discussions and the other entertainment, so the vote was pretty weighted.

The children had long days. They were in school until four in the afternoon, after which they had chores and home-work and, of course, dinner. Generally, in the evening, the television aired a half-hour continuing novella, similar to our soap operas, only these ended every six to eight weeks, then another started up. After that, there was usually a movie. It was rare that any of the children, particularly the two younger ones, were allowed to stay up for the film.

However, what could I say one spring evening when the movie, "Sleeping Beauty" was advertised for a school night? The children begged. "I've been good," "I'm getting straight A's," "I'll do my chores right after school, honest." I'd been accused of it, but truly I wasn't an ogre. What could I say? Besides, I wanted to see it, too.

With all the willing hands and happy faces, the chores were done, dinner was eaten without the usual arguments or complaints, dishes were shining and dry and four eager chil-dren and one expectant adult settled happily in front of the television.

The music started, credits and title ran against a back-drop of woods with the spires and crenellated towers of a hidden castle rising into wisps of mist. Five pairs of eyes gazed at the screen as a group of footmen arrived leading their mounts. The handsome prince, dressed in white dou-blet and hose, a magnificent white feather curling under his chin, was mounted on a prancing white stallion.

Then the camera panned to the forest, where wood nymphs flitted from tree to tree trailing diaphanous veils. Suddenly, the footmen dropped their reins, as well as their pants, and chased after the nymphs. The veils were quickly dispatched and the nymphets were totally revealed. And I mean totally. This was not a Disney production.

"Okay, kids, bedtime." I overcame my shocked paralysis and flicked off the set just as Prince Charming dismounted. And disrobed. This wasn't what I'd agreed to. This sort of education could wait. The kids were laughing too hard to argue.

The next morning, still chuckling over the film fiasco, I was making breakfast for the children when I heard Wendy's agitated voice.

"Mom! Mom! She's gone! We gotta find her!" Wendy came leaping down from her room up in the attic. She had decided very quickly that family togetherness in the area of dormitory-sleeping was not to her liking and had scouted out the old attic/grainery directly above the old house and opening onto the hill, which rose steeply behind the buildings. Pointing out the lack of insulation, the broken floorboards just inside the entryway and the great gaping holes around the ancient door, failed to diminish her interest. It was private, it had its own entrance and it would be hers alone. That means a lot to the oldest child in a family of four.

We had swept out the accumulated dust and rat droppings and created a welcoming corner near the windows under the eaves. She retired in blissful privacy with her two spoiled cats and a dog kennel containing Thumper, a big, brown rabbit. The cats were free to come and go at will by squeezing through the broken floorboards and exiting under the door. At night or whenever Wendy was away from her haven of peace, Thumper was put in the kennel.

Except, that is, for the previous night, when, unknown to me, Thumper had settled down so happily in a corner under the eaves that Wendy hadn't the heart to disturb her. The rabbit was sweet and tame; she played games with the children and with the cats and came when her name was called. So tame, in fact, that we half expected her to come in with the cats for breakfast that morning.

However, by the time I took the children to school, and in spite of repeated calling all around, through the barns, up the hillside, into the woods, Thumper had not appeared and Wendy was near tears. I assured her that I would continue the search during the day and that Thumper would surely return home soon.

For the next week, Wendy's first move upon returning home after school, even before checking out the contents of our newly acquired refrigerator, was running to her room calling Thumper's name. And every morning she leaped up, checking the bowls of feed and water for signs of Thumper's presence. To no avail. No bunny.

By the second week, we were trying to think positively of Thumper's new existence in the wild, enjoying the lush greenery, the companionship of the wild rabbits. Maybe she even had a boyfriend. We didn't mention the fox.

Saturday morning, we had just finished breakfast when an elderly couple strolled into the courtyard. He had grey hair and a distinguished countenance which beamed good humor and, though he carried a walking stick, certainly had no need of it for walking. She was smaller and wider with shining white hair and a big smile and carried a basket over her arm.

"Bon jour, Madame, les enfants," they called out in unison. "Please allow us to introduce ourselves. We are the Saint-Martins, your neighbors up through those trees." M'sieur Saint-Martin had taken over as spokesman.

"Does this, by any chance, belong to you?" Madame Saint-Martin raised the cloth covering the basket. Two brown ears popped up followed by the bright eyes of Thumper.

Wendy shrieked with joy and pulled the big rabbit into her arms, heading for her room.

"Eh oui! On en etait certaine." M'sieur and Madame Saint-Martin smiled happily. "When we went out to our garden and saw this lovely *lapine*, who did not run away, but hopped eagerly over to us for petting, we knew she did not belong to any of our other neighbors. She could only have come from here." Madame Saint-Martin was beaming with joy at her deductive powers.

M'sieur Saint-Martin was retired from the S.N.C.F. *(Societé Nationale de Chemins de Fer)*, the railroads, and had also sung with the Bordeaux Opera. Madame was a retired school principal. The two had bought their property at the top of the hill, which they were in the process of restoring, explaining that it was a *gentilhommerie*. A chateau, apparently, has round turrets, whereas their home had a square one.

"It is us who protect you from the winds," M'sieur said. "We are at the top of the hill and the wind blows from all sides. You, on the other hand, sit just below the hilltop and have the view without the wind."

They left with our expressions of gratitude, Madame's promise to bring us her special *tarte aux châtaignes* as soon as the chestnuts came in season and an invitation to dinner. A delightful pair, who began and ended each other's sentences, never interrupting yet both seeming to speak simultaneously. I couldn't wait to visit them at the *gentilhommerie*.

Joining Wendy in her lair, I petted Thumper and noted that she didn't appear to have missed many meals during her absence. Of course, the Saint-Martin's garden wasn't exactly "life in the wild."

The following week, Wendy commented on Thumper's heavy shedding, which appeared strange for this time of year.

"Don't they shed like cats, you know, in the hot summer? At least she's neat about it. She's put all the old hair in one big pile."

Oh-oh, I thought. *Thumper had company.*

Yep. Thumper had eloped and had a fling with a wild bunny and returned home in the family way. In another week, the soft nest of brown and white fur wiggled; ten days after that six tiny blind infants staggered out. We moved the little family into new hutches on the protected north wall of the hay barn and kept them well supplied with fresh alfalfa and rabbit food.

The babies grew rapidly, but never attained Thumper's size. Nor the length of her ears. They were small, with shorter ears and longer hind legs, although they had their mother's lovely brown and white coloring. They didn't appear to have inherited their mama's calm disposition, however, and whizzed round and round their hutch when anyone approached.

I have no idea whether this fact has any physiological significance, but none of the females ever reproduced. However, Trompette, the lone male, gained a neighborhood reputation as a stud and, since the wild taste was a local gourmet preference, his services were often requested. He never failed and was always happy to oblige!

❧ CHAPTER 14 ❧

La Truffe

Fall had come again. The sun was still shining but without its summer heat, the breeze forecasted frost, clouds drifting like dried sage across a desert floor, song birds long since departed for homes in the palms. In the air was a sense of regret for something I could not quite identify.

I'd taken the kids to school, picked up my morning-fresh loaf of bread and was huddled in the kitchen over a *café au lait* with a warm, crusty chunk slathered with creamy butter when the dogs announced an arrival. Short, skinny and furtive, the man was wearing a brown, moth-eaten woolen stocking cap, pulled well over his ears. If I'd been in the market, I'd have clutched my purse close to my chest. He wore a long, brown sweater with patches on the elbows—right next to the holes—and he was accompanied by a brown terrier with short, pointy ears who was barking insults at Penny and Schultz from the shelter of his master's bowed legs.

I stepped outside, calmed the dogs and shook the man's extended hand, tempted to count my fingers when I got them back. At this stage, I understood up to five words out of every ten, so I think he introduced himself and told me he had been doing something on my property for so many years he practically had Napoleonic rights. What he'd been doing wasn't too clear.

The little, weather-browned man had an unfortunate habit. He sniffed. After every third word. And with every few sniffs, he dragged the sleeve of his ragged sweater across his face. This didn't help my comprehension a bit.

Then he reached into the dirty bag slung over his shoulder and pulled out a muddy, black object which resembled nothing more than a charred wart. It was about the size of a walnut and he handled it like a Fabergé egg. Reverently and with obvious, deep regret, he handed it to me.

The thing sat in my open hand like an obscene lump and I regarded it with distaste. *"Qu'est ce que c'est?"* I inquired.

"Ça va, Ça va." He dug further into the grubby bag and pulled out another, then glancing sideways at me, a third smaller one and handed me the lot. Apparently I had just bartered him out of more of the rare and disgusting objects.

I stood there with the three dirty black warts resting on my hand as he sniffed twice, mumbled what I assumed were the traditional words of parting, swiped his sleeve across his face, whistled for his dog and ambled off down the lane. Strange people, these French.

My coffee was well chilled by now, so I placed the lumps on the kitchen window ledge and headed out to work on the fences. With two horses and a couple of calves on the property, the fence lines needed major work. Problem was, there seemed to be miles of the things and the end was nowhere in sight.

Hunger, cold feet and a need to replenish my supply of ceramic wire insulators drove me back to the house in the early afternoon, just as Gabriel's car came rattling down the lane.

"*Salut, Janine. Ça va?*" Gabriel was never one to stand on ceremony and he walked inside heading for the kitchen. Within minutes, he was pouring a couple of glasses of wine. Formality never kept him from the wine stash either.

Just then I detected a strong odor of something rotten and was earnestly searching for a morsel of old cheese as the most likely culprit. Gabriel, however, inhaled deeply and went into an almost devout trance.

"*Les truffes. Où sont-elles? Ah-h-h-h...*" Gabriel leaped at the ugly lumps on the windowsill and reverently breathed their fragrance, admired their size and held them with the gentleness of a new father.

I described the visit of the raggedy little man and Gabriel erupted in rage. "*Merde! Espêce de salaud! Voleur!*" He never became inarticulate when angered. *Au contraire*, he spoke clearly and distinctly and followed with a dissertation on the man's maternal antecedents and other barnyard relatives. I waited patiently for the end, making mental notes of a few of the epithets, hoping to find them in my dictionary. I didn't think I should mention them to the boys.

When calm had been regained with the help of another *coup de rouge*, some deep breathing and a lot of muttering, Gabriel patiently explained the situation and the history of my odoriferous, dirt-encrusted black warts, otherwise known as truffles.

Truffles, *les truffes,* are fungi. In a country of gas-
tronomes, where smell and taste bud satisfaction rank right
up there with other orgasmic treats, the *truffe* is regarded
with awe and reverence. It is created only by God. No attempt
by man has yet succeeded to grow the unlovely objects in
selected locations. They simply cannot be farmed. They
choose certain oaks, preferring ones of great venerability,
and shyly settle themselves down amongst the roots.

Their presence is detected by smell. As already noted,
the odor is pungent and distinct. Pigs have a particular talent
for unearthing the black lumps of fungal gold. The drawback
with using pigs to root out truffles lies in the fact that once
they detect the unique aroma, they lust for the taste of l*a
truffe*. And restraining one hundred twenty pounds of sali-
vating, truffle-hungry hog is not all that easy. Then dogs were
brought into the picture. Dogs could be trained to not eat the
treasure. Many dogs have shown great talent for *truffe*-detec-
tion. In our little corner of the world, the weather-beaten
man's dog had a remarkable reputation.

Les truffes, found only in locales of their own discrim-
inating selection, appear to have settled upon the Pèrigord as
their natural home. I can understand that. Particularly since
plumbing and electricity were not among their requirements
for comfortable living.

In spite of a rather overpungent odor in its natural
state, the *truffe* adds a delicate, incomparable flavor when
small morsels are added in the preparation of certain foods.
An omelette, for instance, moves out of the category of
scrambled eggs and becomes the object of an assignation,
something to be served with a fine, chilled champagne by
candlelight. *Pâté*, poultry stuffing—the list is limited only by

the imagination of the chef. It is said that a single truffle placed in a barrel of eggs, still in their shells, is sufficient to flavor each egg in the barrel. I believe it. They certainly flavored my entire kitchen.

All of this combines to put the truffle right up there with the diamond when setting a value. I've never met a South African diamond trader. But I had now met a truffle trader, a *truffier*. Gabriel informed me that the current market value of these ugly black warts was about 2,000 francs per kilo, or four hundred dollars. I considered digging up every oak on the property, but decided that was not only impractical, it was comparable to killing the golden, egg-laying goose.

So Gabriel consented to share with me the third method, after pigs and dogs, of finding *les truffes*. Of course, I had to agree to let him have the occasional one or two. The method was...trained flies.

On a sunny day, one lurks around the trunk of a known truffle oak, of which we had at least two at *Vezat*, observing flies. Prod lightly around the base of the tree with a stick and if a fly hovers, dig in that spot—gently, fingers only, pausing to smell the soil. If the aroma of a *truffe* is detected, further digging is merited.

The word was spread to the *truffier* and his dog that *Vezat* was off limits for his activities. However, after several afternoons spent hanging around the oaks communing with flies, I crossed off another possibility for making our fortune. Later I discovered that the gift of a small, ugly black fungus was a wonderful way to be assured of an invitation to a gourmet dinner and an evening in the company of warm, genial friends. That was sufficient fortune for me.

PART 2

Les Aventures et Les Dure Épreuves

An inconvenient family.
We could have been shipped out to sea,
or rocketed to the moon,
one sunny day in June.

Our love was expendable,
fully amendable,
not too commendable.

Instead we were emigrated,
which is like being sequestrated,
only somewhere else. Far else.

We reappeared on a farm in France
by happenchance.
No hot and cold, no lights, no toilet,
in other words, not spoiled.

But critters plenty, cows and sheep,
and things that peep
and peck and grow and need.
Life continues—filling, swelling,
overwhelming.

Love should be returned by love,
need and caring hand-in-glove.
His loss.

Inconceivably, irretrievably,
an inconvenient family.

❦ CHAPTER 15 ❧

An Inconvenient Family

Rob didn't get over for Christmas that year. He wrote that the printing company had some major contract deadlines and was in a fight for survival. He said he still hoped to avoid a bankruptcy. It was late summer when he finally arrived, nearly a year since his last visit.

Our excitement was uncontainable. The kids were like bubbles bursting around a water pipe. His lips brushed my face and he suggested we have dinner out, by ourselves.

We went to the *Hotel Restaurante* in the nearby village of Meyrals, a charming spot located in the middle of a small wood. The restaurant opened out to a deck, covered by latticework over which grew an enormous grapevine, dripping huge bunches of ripening fruit directly over the tables. A symphony of crickets harmonized from the darkness, with an occasional frog joining in on the bass. A light breeze carried the scents of pine from the forest mingled with sautéeing garlic.

We sat at a table on the terrace, enjoying the balmy evening and immediately ordered the house wine, which came in an earthenware pitcher. The house wines in the local restaurants were of universally good quality, coming as they did from the best of the nearby vineyards, untouched by preservatives or chemicals.

Lately, I'd spent my waking hours looking, and probably smelling, like a farmhand. That night I wore a soft turquoise linen sheath. My long hair, usually pulled into a ponytail, was caught from both sides by a large barrette on the back of my head and fell in brushed waves onto my shoulders. I smelled great. And felt like a woman.

Ordering was not a problem. As in many small restaurants in rural France, the menu was without choice. You ate what the chef prepared. Certainly not a problem as the meals were always good. Still, Rob looked nervous as he fidgeted with his wine glass.

A plate of *pâté truffé* appeared on the table, along with a basket containing chunks of bread from the local *boulangerie.* They were noted for their large round wheels of bread, dark and crusty.

I held up my glass of wine to toast our being together again, but Rob's glass was already at his lips, his eyes turned toward the surrounding trees. I felt a chill in the air and shivered. My joy in the evening suddenly felt tenuous. I was tasting the *pâté* when chilled plates containing slivered slices of cucumber, tomato and hardboiled egg sprinkled with fresh herbs and lightly covered with vinaigrette were placed in front of us.

Rob put his fork down and blurted out, "We—I—need to talk. I haven't been fully honest with you. I—I've met someone else; she's a lot like you, you know, that's what attracted me." His eyes were firmly fixed on the wine as he swirled the glass. "I guess I don't have your strength."

All the suspicious signs I had for so long repressed flooded into my mind. "Were you seeing her before we left the States?" I asked quietly, sounding much calmer than I actually felt. It was necessary to press him; I wasn't about to swallow more lies.

"Yes." He tossed back the wine and grabbed for the pitcher. "I didn't think you knew."

"I...I guess I did."

The lump in my throat made it difficult to talk. Some people become eloquent under stress, fight for their lives—or their marriages—with words and phrases formed in the heart and spoken in husky, emotion-filled voices. I was struck dumb, with a bowling ball lodged smack over the vocal chords.

Rob was making deep inroads on the wine pitcher. Did he imagine that numbing his brain would ease my pain? Or was it just easier for him that way?

"It's not that I don't love you. You must understand that. I'll always love you and the kids. But I can't give her up. I love her too. Surely you can understand."

No, I couldn't—wouldn't—understand. We weren't just the two of us. We were a family.

"Do you want a divorce?" I didn't recognize the flat, too-high sound emerging from my throat. Tears dripped down my face, thoroughly salting the food in front of me. The chef would be furious.

The waiter appeared again with steaming plates of *escalopes de veau,* thinly sliced veal covered with slices of mushrooms in a light wine-flavored sauce. At the side were dark green asparagus spears. He deftly removed the barely-touched plates of *cruditées vinaigrettes,* glanced at my tear-stained, devastated face and discreetly disappeared.

"Yes—probably—not right away. I'll always take care of you, of course. All of you. You know that, don't you?" Rob's speech sounded strained and rushed, as if he had to get all the words out quickly and be done with it.

How could I possibly believe that he would always take care of us when he'd been lying to us for years? He had deposited his wife and children in a Utopian landscape, far from the problems in a violence- and drug-prone urban America, but also devoid of the modern conveniences found there. He'd said he was returning to the States to settle his affairs. "Settling his affairs" apparently meant forming a new life with her, whoever she was, and that was, basically, that. I guess he figured *they* could cope with society's ills. I think they embodied them.

Looking down, I cut a bite of the tender meat, then pushed it around my plate. I had already started eating the European way with fork in left hand and knife in right. It felt terribly cosmopolitan. Besides, it made sense. But, since I wasn't eating, it was stupid to hold the utensils at all. I laid them beside my plate and gazed off into the distance where the woods soon grew blurry then dissolved behind a curtain of tears. My tears wouldn't stop, nor would that damned bowling ball go away.

Quickly, I pushed away my plate and stood up. My chair toppled over.

"Please." Again that unrecognizable voice. "Please, take me home."

The farm was quiet and the children blessedly asleep. Or, if not, they were clever enough to pretend. I felt the bowling ball within my throat expand as I thought of telling them. Then I drew the blinds in my mind. Tomorrow.

Rob and I prepared for bed silently. The last time we would share a bed. Was I innocent? Deluded? Stupid? I'd always pictured "wicked" as a delicious mischief. Now I knew wicked intimately. It wasn't delicious.

We slipped into bed, each clinging to an opposite edge. I listened to my heart breaking, my dreams cracking and whispered, "I can't do this. I won't make it."

"Why not?" His voice was suddenly defensive and angry. I wasn't acting the way he'd expected. I wasn't being reasonable. "I said I'd take care of you. You and the kids will be fine. What can't you do?"

I felt an emptiness inside that I was sure could never be filled again. I struggled to speak as tears drenched my pillow.

"I still love you," I finally whispered. The words floated in the air then disappeared. Rob made no response.

Through the open window, I heard the old walnut tree brushing the roof, felt the soft breeze. Nocturnal critters rustled in the leaves, *cigales* chirrupped. The unbroken silence of the room echoed with the light, familiar sounds. Only I was different.

✤ CHAPTER 16 ✤

What Color
Was My Parachute?

When the first colored rays of dawn tinted the morning sky, I was sitting in the window staring out. Those three-foot deep stone windows were an ideal spot for reflecting, if a bit hard on the nether regions. I had no recollection of how long I had been sitting there. Nor what I was reflecting upon. My mind had quite simply shut down. Actually, I was surprised that the sun was rising. At the very least, it could have waited a respectful interval or produced thunder and lightning or rain or fat grey clouds. But no, the sky became a shimmering blue as far as forever and the birds were sweetly warbling as always.

I couldn't really see much since my eyes were nearly swollen shut and the view through the slits was blocked by my matted lashes. I've read books in which the heroine, after a night of weeping, regards the world with "eyes sparking with unshed tears" and gazes "through dewy lashes." Her cheeks are either "alabaster pale with pain" or "rosily flushed with emotion." In my case, my eyes were red and swollen, my nose puffy and stuffed and my entire face blotched as if afflicted with some plague from the Middle Ages. None of this did much for my self-esteem.

"How are you going to tell the kids?" Rob asked in a somber monotone. He was sitting on the far side of the bed, turned away from me. I guess Rob hadn't slept too well either. Or the bird's singing had filtered through his dreams. Now I was going to filter in another hard cold fact.

"Me!" I said. "How am I going to tell the kids? I'm not. I figure they'll be getting up pretty soon, so why don't you take yourself down to the kitchen, fix everyone some scrambled eggs and toast and then proceed to ruin their day? This is *your* news. *You* can tell them. I'll be with the horses." I pulled on jeans and a sweatshirt, shoved my feet in sneakers and left.

In the big barn, I grabbed a bale of hay and divided it into the two mangers, as Bambi and Étoile whickered good morning. Then I grabbed a couple of buckets and put in a scoop each of grain. I don't know why I felt the horses needed comfort food, but it made me feel better. Then, while they ate, I groomed them. I brushed and combed and muttered and whimpered. Bambi munched and whickered and lipped my shoulders and head, as though he knew I was in need of comforting. He was a wonderfully sympathetic and loving animal. At least when you talked to him. When you got on his back and expected him to behave like a proper horse, it was a different matter.

Bambi, I had decided, was simple-minded. Or else he really didn't like doing horse things, like going around with a rider on his back. I usually rode early in the morning before turning him out to graze. One time we had taken the dirt road in back of the farm which wound through the woods and over the hill. I think it might have been a fire access road and hunters used it a lot during hunting season.

Anyway, he kept trying to turn off the road and head into the woods and I was constantly pulling him back onto the path. I'd learned to ride Western style, in which you lay the rein across the neck on the opposite side you want to turn. Bambi had evidently learned English style, in which the rein is pulled on the side you want to turn into. I'd resorted to using both styles to haul that stubborn blockhead around. At one point, his head was facing one direction, his body traveling the other when the reins suddenly broke off at the bit. There I sat, dumbfoundedly holding two strips of useless leather, one in each hand. It took both of us a couple of minutes to figure out what had happened. I spent my time looking for a soft spot to land on, one which would cause the least amount of pain, while Bambi spun around and headed home.

Then there was the mailbox. Our mailbox was nailed to an oak tree at the junction of our lane with the communal road. Bambi was terrified of it. I don't know what he expected it to do, but over time his terror never abated. Not even after years in which the mailbox never moved, never made a sound and certainly never threatened a single passerby, man or beast, did he conquer his panic.

I had to lead him gently past the oak tree with the affixed mailbox, talking softly, putting myself between him and the Terror, preferably even turning his head so that the sight of this Awful Thing wouldn't cross his wildly rolling eyes. Once past, I could mount and he would happily prance off up the road.

On one of Rob's prior visits, he'd noticed me leading Bambi down the lane before mounting and asked me why. Embarrassed, I explained the situation.

"Oh for heaven's sake! That's ridiculous! You'll never train that animal if you continue to cater to him." He was right, of course, but Bambi had turned out to be more stubborn even than me.

Rob jumped on Bambi's back in the lane and trotted him right out to the oak tree and mailbox, whereupon Bambi reared up and Rob rapidly slid off his backside. Did I mention that I usually rode bareback?

Rob walked up, grabbed Bambi's reins and, with a hand clutching his mane, leaped right back up onto his back, turned him around and forced him toward the Evil Monster. Again, Bambi reared up and Rob slid down.

Tim and I stood to the side watching and trying very hard not to giggle. It wasn't funny. Really, it wasn't. Unfortunately, we had to turn our backs and silently shake. We wiped our eyes, composed our faces and turned around to see Rob back up on the horse, his hand firmly gripped high on Bambi's mane, again forcing him by the Vicious Beast. Bambi reared up and Rob held on, attempting to kick from a nearly vertical position. Bambi slowly lowered himself to a sitting position and proceeded to roll onto his back as Rob, rather hastily, stepped off the side.

"You've ruined him, you know," he said, handing me the reins.

However, in the barn that morning, Bambi was sweet and gentle. He was deeply concerned that I was upset and I reveled in his concern. I have very little memory of that day. I may have hidden out in the barn all day, I simply don't recall.

Jill told me later that when her father had told her we were separating, she couldn't stop crying and Tim gave her an old Halloween mask to wear so no one would see the tears. She wore that mask for several days.

One of the boys asked me, "Mom, what's going to happen to us?"

I hugged him and said, "Sweetheart, you have me forever."

"It's not your fault," I kept reassuring them. "It's mine. It's only me he doesn't love."

Rob left for the United States soon thereafter. "I have to get away to think," he insisted. I didn't know what there was left to think about.

CHAPTER 17

Tough Decisions

In one of the children's science books, I found a picture of the human heart, which showed it divided into four chambers, like a four-room house. I discovered that's not exactly true. The heart has little side rooms where you can dump things you don't want to think about and close the doors, junk rooms, *la poubelle*. Only the doors are more like curtains, because sometimes, when you least expect it, a gust of wind blows one open and you see that thing you didn't want to think about and you fall apart all over again. Then you tuck the curtain down nice and tight one more time and hope the wind won't blow for awhile.

When I finally got the curtain in place and accepted Rob's permanent departure, I figured some decisions needed to be made. Despite my reluctance to add to their pain, I had to speak to the kids. After all, this didn't concern just me.

"We need to talk, guys," I said quietly, hoping my voice sounded calm and confident. "We need to make some decisions and I thought we should approach this democratically. This is our family and we need to work things out together and decide if we should go back home."

Wendy was visibly upset. "Mom, I'm tired of moving. I didn't especially want to leave New Jersey, but we did. Now I want to stay here. I've got friends and everything. And no one even knows we're not French until *you* open your mouth."

The others agreed wholeheartedly with Wendy. I breathed a sigh of relief and didn't even take offense at the crack about my accent. I'd been prepared to assert dictatorial powers if they'd voted any other way, but the democratic forum had worked. Our accommodations, though something less than luxurious, had become familiar and felt like home and the last thing in the world we wanted was to move again. Besides, the magic had been insidiously working away and we all kind of liked it here.

I must admit that at a time like this, distance and isolation is not a bad thing. While I hadn't the dubious comfort of commiserating friends agreeing that my husband was an absolute bastard and that I was a poor, brave darling, the crushing humiliation of rejection and failure was easier to deal with alone on a farm in a remote area of a foreign country.

The radical change in our lives had actually begun, I now realized, a couple of years before. For two years I had dug my head firmly into the sand, resolutely neither seeing nor hearing anything that might turn my well-ordered life into chaos. Not that it wasn't already—chaotic, that is. Actually, it's hard to believe I considered it well-ordered.

Heaven knows, I was literally battered about the head and shoulders with hints that all was not as it should be in a normal husband and wife relationship. However, a head buried as deeply as mine simply does not feel these batterings. Or, at the very least, gives no outward signs of being aware.

We'd been deposited on a three-hundred-year-old farm with suitcases, dogs and numerous panic attacks while Rob stayed in Washington to tend to business...or whatever. I refused to dwell on her—The Whatever. In truth, we'd never been too accustomed to Rob spending much time with the family. He traveled a lot and worked the rest of the time. It was just that he was *there*. You know, "I'll ask Dad what he thinks when he calls," or "Oh, Dad'll be so proud," or "Well, we'll see. I'll have to ask Dad."

Although I felt betrayed, I tried to concentrate on the positive aspects of being on our own. Suddenly, I'd been promoted to Top Dog. I didn't have to ask for anyone's permission or ideas or approval. Of course, I had only me to make it work. And there wasn't anyone there holding a safety net. If I fell, there'd be only the hard, cold ground underneath, probably loaded with rocks. Well, I told myself, I couldn't say that my marriage had turned out to be a bed of roses either.

So that the children would be spared my emotional turmoil, I took some time out, spending many evenings out in the field under the big oak, talking it over with the horses. They'd come over and run their big velvety noses across my arm and whuffle a bit until I pushed them off. I also talked to the four cows we'd acquired, two black and whites which we'd bought at the same time as the horses and who were going on two years old and two *Limousines*, big red beef cows we'd raised from calves with the others. The black and whites were sweet and friendly, but not the other two. One was skittery and nervous and the other would just as soon skewer me on her big curved horns as look at me.

On one of my cathartic visits, the aggressive *Limousine* began watching me through heavy-lidded, brown eyes. As time passed, she seemed to grow agitated and began pawing the ground with her hooves. As I leaned against a tree watching the horses, she gave a few snorts, then one bellow and took off after me. That cow just tucked her head down and charged. All I had to see were those big, curved horns zooming toward me and I ran. I ran faster than I thought I could and hurtled over three wires of electric fence, a feat that, I felt with some pride, would have won me a spot on any Olympic broad jump team.

It was that fickle personality thing which finally made me think that maybe raising beef cattle wasn't going to be the answer to our money problem. That and the pure, cold logistics of how many cows could be raised on how much space and for how long before they made a profit. As my new, solitary state went on, money was getting scarcer and scarcer. Rob said the fortunes of the printing company had spiraled downward, along with the value of the property in Maryland that Rob had bought for his ladylove.

By then my pain was pretty well sealed off in that little room in my heart and I began to get mad. Damn! If he didn't want me, I sure as hell wasn't going to continue to be a financial burden. Rob had a responsibility to his children, but I was damned if I was going to be another one. Not if I could help it. I just had to figure out how to turn fifty acres into a paying proposition.

And that's when it came to me. Milk cows. I'd raise milk cows. Surely I could learn how. Half the folks around us did it and if they could do it, I could. I talked it over with the children and they agreed to help. We all filed away our day-dreams of faithful family retainers mucking out stalls into the folders marked fantasy. Taking a deep breath, I set about learning a new trade.

My first task, the moment I told him, was getting Gabriel to stop laughing. As the boys put it, he just about "split a gut" when I first brought up the subject. I wasn't ready to drop the fiction of my happy-though-separated-by-distance marriage, so I explained there were financial problems at Rob's printing company. Gabriel had trouble getting his mind around the idea of an American who wasn't rich by virtue of nationality, but I finally persuaded him, at least, to teach me the rudiments of milking.

That afternoon at milking time, Tim and I headed up to the nearby farm of Gabriel's uncle and walked into the tiny barn. This was nothing like the Rougier spread. The barn was dirt floored, but raked clean, with fresh straw underfoot. The area was so dark I had to wait a minute to let my eyes adjust. A false floor had been run at a height just overhead, covering three-fourths of the barn. This loft was filled to the rafters with hay. The first stall inside the door contained the fattest pig I'd ever seen. At the moment, it was slurping with enormous gusto at a mushy pile of stuff I didn't want to examine too closely.

"C'est Pompidou. Il est beau, non?" Gabriel called over his shoulder from where he was milking a big black and white cow. He was commenting on the beauty of the pig. All the villagers, I had noticed, seemed to name their beasts for political figures, past and present. A form of compliment, no doubt.

L'oncle, pitchfork in hand, stepped out shyly from behind another cow. Tall and slender, he walked crouching, to avoid the low ceiling. He murmured *"B'n j'r"* and barely touched my hand, bobbing and weaving, never quite meeting my eyes. Hard to believe this man, dying in an agony of timidity, could be related to Gabriel. *L'oncle* was much more comfortable clapping Tim on the shoulder in a man-to-man gesture.

"Eh ben, Janine, on trait?" Gabriel chuckled happily as he moved off the stool beside the cow, still pulling strongly and directing a steady stream of milk into the bucket. *"Mettez les mains là."* He indicated that I should move my hands over his and take over the milking.

I took his place on the stool, moved my hands into position as Gabriel slid his hands out and pulled just like he did. Only the milk stopped flowing. I pulled harder. Nothing. Hearing the rattle of the heavy chain collar, I looked up and saw an astonished cow face peering back at me. Gabriel's hearty laughter didn't help a bit.

He moved back in and re-started the flow. Again I took over and...nothing. Gabriel placed his hands over mine to demonstrate the technique and the milk started again, pinging against the side of the bucket. I moved my smaller hands up and down to imitate the motion, beginning to feel like I was getting it, when he removed his hands and...oh damn! No more ping.

"Hey, Mom, let me try," Tim pulled on my sleeve.

The very least Tim could have done was start slowly. But no, the minute he sat down and placed his eleven-year-old hands on that cow, the milk resumed its steady flow, and the cow went back to eating contentedly. The brat even aimed a stream at the barn cat sitting off to the side, hitting her mouth without spilling a drop. Gabriel laughed harder.

On the ride home, Tim tried to make me feel better. "It's okay Mom. Danny and I can milk the cows for you," he said grinning broadly. "You just do the rest of the stuff, you know, mucking out barns and taking care of the calves."

I knew he was trying to cheer me up. But it wasn't helping. I decided I'd just keep trying. After all, I wouldn't have to worry about actually milking until I had actual milk cows. I had two who were within days of being just that, but our dairy operation was nowhere near ready for them. How those two cows had gotten themselves into that condition is rather pertinent.

One afternoon, nine months earlier, we drove into the courtyard on the after school run. Tim ran to the fence and hollered, "Mom, look at all the cows in the field. Are they ours?"

Sure enough, the field was crowded with about a dozen big red cows. Our two fifteen-month-old *hollandaises* were being tenderly shepherded by a large, heavily muscled red cow. Startled, I did a double take. No, wait a minute, no cow I ever saw came equipped like that. He was magnificently endowed and ready for action. And act he did, at regular intervals, with first one of my young ladies and then the other. With their full cooperation.

I was angry enough to stomp out into the field and yell at him, when he turned and gazed at me—that's all, he just looked at me with his head slightly lowered. And I hightailed it. I might have been a little dumb, but even I knew enough not to mess with a bull. Especially not a bull in love.

Danny was tugging my arm, trying to get my distracted attention.

"Mom, Mom, Mom! I think I know who he belongs to. Paul, a kid in my class, well his dad has cows on the farm just below ours. He said they had a bull. I bet it's him. And the cows, too."

Dan took off on his bike, pedaling furiously toward his friend's home, while we did evening chores and tried to ignore the red menace in the field with our pampered darlings who didn't even have the grace to object.

The sun had set and dusk was oozing into total darkness by the time the headlights of a car cut into the courtyard. Danny bounced out, followed by three other men, and pulled his bike out the back of the small white van. He introduced M'sieur Charbonnel, who then presented the older man, his father-in-law, and a tall youth in his late teens, his son Luc.

"Alors, où est ce rascal, Zeus?" M'sieur Charbonnel was tall and slender, with a shock of curly black hair and laughing blue eyes. I tried really hard to maintain my righteous anger and made some comment about the danger of a crazy bull attacking my young girls. He chuckled and assured me that his bull was too well-mannered to visit unless he was invited first and that it was probably the girls who made the first pass. While I fumed, he walked out in the field toward his menacing beast, cooing *"gros minou"* as the huge animal dropped its head and rubbed it against his shirt front and he scratched lovingly behind the big ears. A big pussycat named for the king of gods! Did I ever feel stupid.

M'sieur Charbonnel started down the field with his arm draped over the monstrous bull's neck, Luc pushed the straggling cows in behind and the father-in-law peeled out my two young hussies and escorted them through the barn door which the boys were holding open. I stood there and continued to feel stupid, then decided I might be more useful by turning off the electric fence so they could pass into their fields and, hopefully, put my fence back together.

And that's the story of how my girls got knocked up. Motherhood was now imminent; however, I soon had an offer for both mamas and their calves from M'sieur Charbonnel's father-in-law. Since I was not yet prepared to go into the dairy business, I kept going back and forth in my mind as to whether or not to accept it.

❧ CHAPTER 18 ❧

A New Career

As time and the seasons passed, I found myself focusing on the future and letting go of the past. In every life change, I came to realize, no matter how negative, there are positives. Perhaps that is what is meant by the old saying, "No bad wind blows."

I loved the early morning hours while the children, who were on school vacation, slept late. Accompanied by the dogs, a cat or two and miscellaneous poultry, I walked down the field toward the woods, looking for the cows and reassessing my plans to become self-sufficient. I really needed to make a decision soon. By my calculations, calving could start in a couple of weeks.

Standing at the edge of the woods, M'sieur Charbonnel smiled at me and beckoned. *"Venez voir,"* he called.

Come see what? I wondered. I ran the rest of the way and there, in the shelter of the trees stood Bessie, my own baby, nudging her wobbly infant with a large raspy tongue. The tiny calf tottered unsteadily, then grabbed a dangling *tetine* with a greedy slurp and sucked out her first meal.

"She's beautiful," I said, marveling at the perfection of the little animal.

"*Eh bien*, and now, have you made your decision to sell to my *beau-père?*"

I shook my head. I had learned that M'sieur Charbonnel maintained a herd of dairy cattle at his home just outside the village, with fields bordering the Dordogne, as well as the herd of *Limousines* which were pastured on the fields below *Vezat*. Aside from the one incident with Zeus, he had been an excellent neighbor, maintaining all the fences that bordered our two properties. He had even volunteered the services of Zeus at the appropriate time for my young *Limousines*. I was beginning to feel an almost in-law relationship to him.

This quiet, pleasant man inspired in me a sense of confidence. He displayed neither inordinate curiosity in us as unique specimens in the neighborhood nor had he made any effort to sell us one of the bridges across the Dordogne River. I decided to share with him my concerns about turning the farm into a paying enterprise and ask his advice. After all, I assured myself, I didn't have to take it.

"*Eh, bien*," he said after some reflection, "you're sure you want to take on the heavy responsibilities of milking? Twice a day, every day, every season, every year, no matter what?"

I assured him that I had given it a great deal of thought, that I saw no alternative and that I would carry it through.

"*C'est vrai,*" he said. "With a property this size, it would create the most consistent income. And you could raise calves also. You have done very well with these."

I accepted the compliment, but then I hung my head and admitted that I had thus far not succeeded in actually milking a cow. Instead of the hearty guffaw I expected, he chuckled lightly. "*Ne vous inquietez pas.* Not to worry. If truth be known, many of our locals would be hard-pressed to milk by hand. It is no longer necessary, nor truly desirable. A machine does a better, quicker and more thorough job." He laughed again. "I think the cows prefer it, too."

He told me of a neighbor who had a small one-cow machine which I could see in operation. He informed me of whom to contact about purchasing a chiller to maintain the milk at the proper temperature. He gave me the name of the butter and cheese company which purchased milk in the area. I felt relieved. He had actually taken me seriously. As if I were a responsible adult, not a crazy American looking for a new hobby.

The dairy business, I told myself, was like any other enterprise. Not to be entered into lightly. Requiring more than just the cows, but also equipment, facilities and a market for the product. But not to be avoided or feared. It was time to quit thinking and start doing.

"Now," he said, "the important thing is to get this cow and her infant taken care of, along with the other one that will not long delay in giving birth. They must be properly milked immediately after giving birth if the milk production is to be brought to maximum levels. If you agree, this is what I propose." And he outlined a plan by which he and his father-in-law would pick up the two cows and the calf later that day and he offered a price I knew to be reasonable.

It turned out that he was in the process of selling off his dairy herd and replacing it with more *Limousines*. He offered to sell me six of his cows, already impregnated, my choice from the herd, as soon as I was ready. This would give me the opportunity to learn the *metier* from cows that already knew the ropes. Much easier than starting with new mamas. The remainder of the herd of ten to twelve, the size herd I had in mind, I would build gradually from my own calves. He, in turn, would purchase my two *Limousines* as they approached their time of calving.

"You are very brave," he said. "This will not be an easy undertaking. Will your husband return soon to help you?"

"Not long," I lied. "My sons will help and the girls also. We can do it. I know we can."

He looked at me, the blue eyes kind and smiling. *"Oui, je croix que vous pouvez."* He thought so too.

My self-confidence was growing. He left me to think over his proposition. I sat down and calculated prices, considered the milking barn and my supplies of feed. We'd had a good haying season and the corn was ripening in the field. There were no guarantees, but then wasn't life itself a crap shoot?

I retrieved my dreams, the ones Rob and I once shared, but realized I had to create new ones, so I shoved the old ones back and concentrated on reality. What else did I need? I had four children who were the sum total of my life. Penny nuzzled my leg and I fondled her soft ear. The calf had finished her first breakfast and settled down in a nest of leaves for a nap. Bessie and her sister moved off and were grazing contentedly with the two *Limousines*. I decided to walk through the woods and up a different field to avoid leaping the fence.

And this afternoon, I decided, I would definitely check out the one-cow milking machine.

❧ CHAPTER 19 ❧

Old Friends and New

Having been raised in a more prudish environment, I had some difficulty at the beginning of my new career discussing the earthier topics common to farmers. After it was explained to me how to tell when a cow is in heat and the need to act promptly to assure her insemination, as that period only lasts one day out of thirty, I spent several days trying to stop blushing from embarrassment.

I soon found out, though, that this becomes an issue of supreme importance with a dairy herd, since production of calves is necessary in the creation of milk. Timing is all.

Among the other lessons I learned was the fact that a resident bull was not only not necessary, but rather a nuisance, unless I wanted to create incestuous relationships. But, not to worry, it could all be taken care of by the artificial inseminator, a man who became known among my kids as "the dirty old man with the long arm." *Eh, oui!*

Needless to say, these topics presented no problems for my children, no bashful blushes, no averting of the eyes. By now, they had become farm kids, knowledgeable and frankly interested.

That spring we acquired a batch of six downy ducklings and raised them under a light bulb in a box in the kitchen. It seemed the only way we could afford meat for our own consumption was to raise it. When the ducklings became full-grown, they had white gleaming feathers, deep full-bodied quacks and an inclination to do everything as a group, as if some of their feathers were interlocked.

The only way to tell the difference between male and female ducks has something to do with whether they have or don't have tail feathers which curl up into a fat sausage curl at the end. I think it's the male which curls and the female which doesn't. The ducks know for sure and that's what's important. But ours didn't seem interested, which struck young Dan and Tim as strange, since the chickens were constantly interested in mating and ducks were sort of distant relatives.

Then one day Danny came home with the solution. "Ducks need water to, um, you know, do it."

We brought out the biggest basin we could find, the one I rinsed clothes in, put the basin in the courtyard and filled it with water. Then we splashed the water to entice the ducks, who came running. Or waddling. Unfortunately, the basin was only big enough for one duck at a time, who swam in an in-place circle quite contentedly until another duck clambered in and on top, but each time she turned in her never-ending circle, he'd fall off her and out of the tub.

It didn't do much for the ducks' libidos, but it sure entertained the kids.

A few days later as I walked out of the *boulangerie*, I heard, "Jan? Jan! Is that you? Oh my God, I don't believe it." The voice came from behind me. I thought I was hallucinating. One doesn't bump into old acquaintances on the streets of a tiny, remote French village. But it was way too early in the day to have been tasting the wine.

I turned around and was caught in an all-enveloping hug. "It is! It's you. I'd heard there was an American family living in the area, but I never dreamed. Oh, I just can't believe it." The dark-haired woman paused for breath and I was able to step back and look.

"Jane. Jane Benson. How wonderful." If my voice was less than enthusiastic, she didn't catch it over her chatter. Jane was the wife of the infamous Bernard Benson who was indirectly responsible for our relocating to France. Very indirectly. I wondered if Rob had spoken to someone who had touted the simple joys of Tibet, Upper Mongolia or Serbia, who knows where we might have landed?

Jane had been Bernard's wife when I worked for him in California and was the mother of his seven children. A mutual friend had written that, after buying his castle in France, Bernard had chucked her for a younger trophy wife. It occurred to me that perhaps we had more in common now than we'd had back in the old days.

"...dinner. You must come to dinner soon. René will want to meet you right away. With Rob and the children, of course."

I tuned back in. René, hmm. Had she met someone?

I went through my usual story about Rob being in the States taking care of business affairs. I had it down pat. Rob and I had agreed that we were irrevocably separated, but that it wasn't necessary to talk about it. Small French villages don't tend to be very broad-minded about divorce, nor about single women living alone. We also decided against mentioning it to Rob's family. He said he needed to wait for the "right time." Could there ever possibly be a right time?

Jane didn't ask any probing questions, probably because she didn't want to be asked any herself. I agreed to bring the children the following evening.

"For you, *Saint Pompon* is practically next door. Just continue up *la Route de St. Zele*, take a left at the top of the hill and we're the second road on the right. Oh, I simply can't wait. How old are the kids now?

I murmured their ages.

"I don't believe it, that's not possible." Another hug, a wave and she was off.

The next evening the children and I drove down a winding, wooded lane that curved around a sweep of pasture harboring a herd of woolly sheep. We pulled to a stop and got out of the car into a small courtyard where we were announced by a huge German shepherd. René bounced out, shushed the dog and greeted us like long-lost family members. He was no taller than me and wore the traditional farmer blues with his beret pushed back on thinning brown hair, a wide smile and the friendly open eyes of a Saint Bernard. I loved him on sight.

It was much later that I noticed he limped and favored his left hand and arm. Deformities on the right side, I later found out, were acquired during a childhood bout of polio. René told me, "If you're not strong, you learn to use your head." By giving no thought to his own physical problems, it seemed, they became invisible to everyone else.

René met Jane shortly after Bernard, in his sweeping expansive fashion, had literally removed her from the chateau they had bought and moved in his *jeune fille*, no older than his oldest daughter. Jane and I appeared to have had equally bad luck in selecting husbands. Mine at least left me my children. But she soon met René, who adored Jane on sight, and shortly thereafter they had purchased *Saint Pompon*, within visiting distance for Jane's children.

I'd forgotten that Jane was a fabulous cook until we walked into the house and were greeted by the aroma of sauces seasoned with garlic and herbs. "When I cook a meal, one eats. When you cook, one feasts," I confessed to Jane. Indeed, this was a joy for all the senses. Taste and smell, of course. Sight, obvious. Even hearing became a sensual treat of sizzling, crackling and the clatter of pans and plates. And touch, even the fingertips recognize the feel of a fork containing *gigot a l'ail* or *lapin a la sauce perigourdine*.

René was in his element as host. I had to stop the wine pouring into the glasses of my sons. Mine, I simply drank. He gossiped non-stop, revealing that he was related to half the community. The other half he either knew personally or through his work as postman. He knew who slept with whom and who wanted to. He knew whose parentage was suspect, along with the who and the why. He knew whose business dealings were shady or downright fraudulent.

René, I soon learned, had the biggest heart in the world. His first question on encountering distress was not "What's wrong?" but "What can I do?" And then he did it. No big deal.

That evening, we worked out a career plan for me, all part of René's using-your-head philosophy. René couldn't drive a car or tractor. He used a left-hand-control *mobylette* for his mailman duties. But he had a lot of muscle packed into a small frame, abundant farm smarts and enough determination to take care of the rest. I, on the other hand, could drive a tractor, but didn't know diddly-poop about farming and suffered a serious lack in the muscle department. Big Business thinks it came up with a whole new concept when it discovered Team Management. We had it in operation in rural France long before.

During the weeks that followed, I cut and raked the hay in the fields of *Vezat* and those at *Saint Pompon*. René carefully consulted the *Farmer's Almanac* before deciding on the fateful day to cut. A *Farmer's Almanac* tells you how many May 3rds in history it has rained in a certain geographical area and gives a percentage possibility for a dry, sunny day. It says absolutely nothing about those big gray clouds massing on the horizon. Whatever, René trusted it—even when it let him down. There was no way I could argue him out of it.

Then we all worked together to bring in the hay. On sunny days, we sang and sweated together. On heavy, rain-threatening days, we worked with speed and economy of motion, trying desperately to beat the storm, for if the cut hay gets wet, the animals won't eat it.

Afterwards we enjoyed *la fête des foins*, our personal celebration for bringing in another field of hay and providing more sustenance for our resident beasts. The dishes were always cooked by Jane, good reason any day for a *fête*.

I plowed our fields and together we sowed the next year's grain crop. I spread fertilizer. We hayed. We were not only a team, we were a family.

René had a hay field located across the road, down a winding trail and split right down the middle by a small stream. The hay grew lush and deep and was a nightmare to cut.

Now the air was thick and soggy, the sun shone white against a sky the color of skim milk. At intervals the far-off, moisture-filled clouds rumbled like an acid stomach. The almanac said warm and sunny. I doubted. René said what did I know. I begged. René announced, *"Demain on fauche."* Tomorrow we cut.

The following morning dawned hot and muggy. The cows were cranky and uncooperative, to my mind a better sign of a change in the weather than René's old almanac. But, as he said, what did I know?

I checked the *faucheuse*, the hay cutter attached on the side of the tractor. All the teeth were firmly in place and the blade freshly sharpened. No more excuses came to mind, so I headed up the hill. Big puffy clouds reared up over the trees. René was waiting at the end of the lane and jumped on the tractor, pitchfork in hand.

"Bonjour, Janine. Quelle bonne journée, n'est-ce pas?" Man, he really believed that stupid book. Beautiful day, my ass. I pointed out the clouds and the air like thick mush, but he just laughed. Nobody was raining on his parade.

We decided to cut the lower half. At least, he wasn't pushing for the whole field. I'd hate to see him lose that much winter feed. I took a sweep around the outer edge while he followed with the pitchfork. The hay was sticky with humidity and a blade not quite sharp enough would have seized up. Mine was cutting through the stalks as if they were warm butter. I stayed well below the creek. The grass was tall, thick and damp where the water ran through.

We'd nearly finished the lower side and I was moving closer to the creek, watching the deep grass like it contained alligators. We hadn't even been aware of the darkening sky, the billowing clouds turning the color of peanut butter or heard the rumblings, but we felt the nuggets striking our backs and heads. Hail as big as golf balls poured down like a hundred golfers gone crazy.

A car horn sounded and Jane's car approached on the far side of the field. René ran toward her and yelled for me to follow. His words were ripped from his mouth and flung to the winds. I decided I could get there just as fast on the tractor, besides getting it out of the field. I continued just below the stream, not thinking what damage the onslaught of rain and hail might be doing to the ground. Risking a face full of ice cubes, I glanced up, just as the right front wheel of the tractor hit a soggy patch and the bank dissolved underneath. The tractor slid slowly and ponderously downward into the creek, first the right front, then the big rear wheel.

Merde! With both feet I jumped off the other side where the mud wasn't quite as deep and ran to the car. Jane tossed me a towel and took off in a roaring reverse back up the hill, hail sounding like machine gun fire on the roof of the car. Within minutes we were dashing through the torrential downpour for the shelter of *Saint Pompon*.

A week later, under a drying sun and with the help of a neighbor, his tractor and a long sturdy chain, we dragged the tractor out of the creek. M'sieur Gorse accused me with a crooked, gap-toothed grin of driving into the creek just to avoid *fauch*-ing the field. With a straight face, I agreed and, when he winked, I felt that I had been granted entry into a private club.

We raked up the ruined hay and stood it in clumps to dry, then hauled it in loose to be used as winter bedding for the animals.

René carefully checked the almanac before we cut the upper field, but I think he sneaked a peek at the sky when I wasn't looking. That night, *la fête des foins* was a particularly joyous party after a successful haying. Later, as I settled down to a well-deserved night's rest, I realized I had rarely in my life felt more satisfaction.

CHAPTER 20

Group Tonsils

That winter was particularly nasty, not cold, just wet. Rain followed by more rain. We'd been delighted to see the precipitation start right after the fall plowings—so good for the soil—but after a while, we were really weary of it. The local expression, *on en a vite marre* (one is quickly fed up), was heard daily.

Wendy was the first one to get sick. Right after Christmas, she came down with a scratchy throat and fever. Dr. DeJean prescribed medication in the form of suppositories.

"He's got to be kidding, Mom. That's gross! No way am I going to put that pill *there*! For one thing, that's not the end that hurts." Wendy was indignant, but when she was finally convinced to follow the doctor's orders, the magic pills actually worked and after a week she was back in school.

Timmy was next. His sore throat and fever was accompanied by a barking cough and drippy nose. Same medication.

Wendy enjoyed picking up the prescription seeing it wasn't for her this time and, once again, the pills worked. About ten days later, Tim was back at the books.

Then it was apparently Danny's turn. For him, any kind of a respiratory ailment turned into asthma and he spent a miserable week wheezing and gasping along with the coughing and sniffing. I'd moved one of the twin beds into the kitchen and it had become our personal hospital ward for the sick-child-of-the-week. Once again, we purchased the miraculous suppositories and both Wendy and Tim enjoyed their brother's horrified reaction. Another ten days and Dan returned to school.

Then Wendy started it all over again. Jill appeared immune, but I barely had time to notice with the other three taking their turns, hacking, sneezing, wheezing and moaning. The suppositories worked in about a week, but had no lasting effect and certainly produced no immunity. Finally, Dr. DeJean announced that their tonsils needed to come out. All three. *En masse.*

Saint-Cyprien had no hospital. Any surgery had to be performed in Sarlat, about half an hour's drive or in Perigueux, an hour's drive. Dr. DeJean made the appointment at a clinic in Perigueux.

"It'll be a breeze," he said. "Kids barely even notice it. A little soreness, but some ice cream will take care of that. And there'll be one big advantage for you," he added with a chuckle. "They'll be pretty quiet for a couple of days."

"How soon can I have ice cream?" asked Danny.

"We'll stop on the way home from Perigueux if you want," I promised.

"What did he mean, we'd be pretty quiet?" asked Wendy.

"I seem to remember that I lost my voice for a couple of days," I responded.

Wendy thought a bit then announced, "Well, I'm not going to."

"Yeah, Wendy'd die if she couldn't talk," the boys chimed in.

Jill was feeling quite left out. The event had taken on a festive air, no one was sick at the moment and suppositories weren't being handed out. I arranged for her to spend T-Day (tonsils day) at *Saint Pompon* where she could help with the baby lambs and a new litter of kittens. She brightened up immediately.

I kept the bed in the kitchen, which had our sole source of heat so my patients could spend their recovery time keeping warm and comfortable. T-Day was a long one. We started early, dropping Jill off with Jane and René, then heading to Perigueux. I was surprised that the clinic hadn't wanted to keep the kids overnight and slightly concerned about driving home three post-surgical kids for an hour and watching them overnight. Nightmarish visions of hemorrhages floated in my mind.

"Nyah, nyah, Wendy's going to lose her voice," the boys chanted together on the drive to the clinic.

"Am not! Am not!" she sang back.

I considered stopping the car and yanking their tonsils out myself.

"Promise we'll stop for ice cream on the way home?" Dan wasn't going to miss out on a treat.

"It's a promise," I said keeping my eye out for an ice cream shop. Luckily I spotted one on the outskirts of Perigueux and made a mental note of its location.

Once we arrived at our destination, we all trooped out
of the car and into the clinic. I was directed to a waiting room
and the children were taken off, gowned and prepared for
the mass surgeries. I settled into a chair in the waiting room
and was surprised when the three operations were completed in a remarkably short time. I was taken to the recovery
room where each was seated in a reclining chair, still groggy.

"Hmmmmmmmmmm." Wendy hummed continually. I
looked questioningly at the doctor. He grinned and said, "I
told her to do that to maintain her voice."

Both boys looked a bit green, but in about an hour,
when everyone was fully awake, I helped them dress and we
headed back to the car. It was already dusk as we started the
return trip, but Danny tugged on my sleeve, beaming a message with his eyes.

"Ice cream?" I asked.

He nodded and I stopped at the little shop I'd spotted
along the way. I purchased three small vanilla cones and
handed one to each child. One small lick was all anyone managed. Soon we were stopping by the roadside to deposit ice
cream for any passing bird with a sweet tooth.

When we arrived home the kids were ready for once
to hit their beds and we headed for the kitchen, now a recovery ward. As the hours passed, I found that Dr. DeJean was
right. The kitchen was quiet, except for continual humming
and rapping as each child pantomimed requests. The boys
were in the bed—one at each end—and Wendy was packed in
blankets in a soft chair. I surrounded them with books,
crayons, cats and dogs. My job was to provide juice, tea with
lemon, soup, ice cream, Jello, etc., etc. upon demand, which
turned out to be almost all the time. After a few days, I was
exhausted.

Though the farm was antiquated and primitive,
the family soon came to love *Vezat's* magic.

In the valley below *Vezat* lies the picturesque
village of Saint-Cyprien and the Dordogne River.

Jan gets ready for a full day on the farm.

Keeping the buildings and grounds of *Vezat* in shape is hard work.

Jan finds out cows that need milking don't like to be kept waiting so she stops only momentarily for this shot.

After the loss of their beloved dachshund, Schultz, Tim and Jill's hearts heal when a new dog, Vicky, enters their lives.

When Tim leaves, Jill gets Vicky all to herself to frolic high atop a pile of hay.

Danny finds friends and adventure going from place to place on his speedy moped.

Though not nearly as fast and exciting as his brother's moped, Tim still has fun on the tractor.

Vicky, the new dachshund, plays with the latest edition to the family, a white Great Pyrenees sheep dog named Jerry.

Jan, Jill and Tim enjoy Jerry's company, unlike the postman, *Bijou*, who is terrified of the big white dog.

During one of their first winters in France, Dan, Jan, Jill and Tim and their pets warm up by the only source of heat—the kitchen stove.

After the loss of their beloved dachshund, Schultz, Tim and Jill's hearts heal when a new dog, Vicky, enters their lives.

When Tim leaves, Jill gets Vicky all to herself to frolic high atop a pile of hay.

Danny finds friends and adventure going from place to place on his speedy moped.

Though not nearly as fast and exciting as his brother's moped, Tim still has fun on the tractor.

Vicky, the new dachshund, plays with the latest edition to the family, a white Great Pyrenees sheep dog named Jerry.

Jan, Jill and Tim enjoy Jerry's company, unlike the postman, *Bijou*, who is terrified of the big white dog.

During one of their first winters in France, Dan, Jan, Jill and Tim and their pets warm up by the only source of heat—the kitchen stove.

For the first time in her entire life, Jill was able to talk without being interrupted. Wendy never lost her voice. She hummed for a couple of days and then spoke in low tones. The boys were back to normal shortly thereafter.

The sun came out, everyone went back to school and I moved the beds back into the bedrooms. Wholesale tonsillectomies and I didn't even get a group rate! I don't know that I'd recommend doing them *en masse*. But, thank heaven, they were over!

✑ CHAPTER 21 ✑

Ladies of the Herd

Many people (usually those who are childless) think children operate on a predictable schedule. Of course, they don't, but kids eventually grow to the point where they sleep late on weekends. Their rhythms slowly change as the seasons and years pass, giving their caretakers needed breaks as well as sporadic frights. However, with the arrival of Olga, Petula and their four sisters, life took on a regular, unchanging, unvaried rhythm, like breathing in and out.

Milk cows, I discovered, arrive each morning at 5:30 A.M. with the regularity of, well, of milk cows eager for breakfast and milking. And again at 5:30 P.M. for dinner and milking. They didn't care a whit whether I'd been out late the night before or up all night with a sick child or was myself alternately shaking with cold and burning up with fever or if I hadn't finished bringing in the hay from the back field and rain was threatening. Their udders were full and they were hungry and, by damn, it was my job to take care of them!

I was fortunate at *Vezat* in having several fields too hilly for cutting hay, as well as large wooded areas, so that I could leave my bovine girls outside year round. Most of my neighbors kept their cows in barns in late fall and winter in order to allow their hay crops to grow, turning the cows out after their first field was cut in the spring. My cows lined up in the field at the courtyard entry and bellowed for service year round.

My girls taught me that cows have a definite hierarchy, a pecking order. Olga was queen of the *troupeau* and always took her undisputed place at the head of the line. This was surprising, since she was also the sweetest, most gentle and least aggressive of the crew. Even her horns curved inward as if to avoid any possible harm to anyone, eventually requiring that they be sawed off to prevent their growing directly back into her skull.

Petula was second in line and she was a different story, with outwardly curving horns and a bitchy disposition. Her udder hung so low that I worried she would step on a dragging *tetine*, causing herself serious damage. Perhaps that was the cause of her attitude. Who knows?

Milk cows are basically docile, as long as they get what they want, and are creatures of habit. Once mine were assigned stall positions, they went to them automatically, munching contentedly at the meal provided. Much of the time, I didn't even bother attaching their chain collars since they wouldn't budge from the spot. Not even during milking.

The little electric one-cow milker recommended to me was, basically, a motor on two wheels with a tall handle for wheeling it around. At the top was a hook, on which hung a round metal cap that fitted tightly on a standard milk *bidon* and a clear plastic hose connecting to four round rubberized suction-type cups. These cups fitted on the cows' *tetines* and sucked the milk out and into the *bidon*. When the milk slowed to droplets in the clear hose and the udder went from the tautness of a water balloon to the looser, flaccid feel of a helium balloon the morning after, the insertion of a finger alongside the *tetine* released the vacuum and the whole works slipped right off, to be hung back on the machine before moving on to the next cow.

The system was kept clean by dunking the four suction cups into a bucket of hot soapy water and running it through the hoses, then rinsing with clear water and hanging to dry. In the winter, I learned to keep the rubberized head and hoses in the kitchen at night if I didn't want to have the entire system frozen solid in the morning. When you live in absolute terror of the mechanized system failing and having to milk by hand, you become fanatic in the care of that system.

I hope the designer of the little one-cow milker received a humanitarian award for his contribution to the world of scientific achievement.

I also learned early in my new career that the French utility companies have no compunction against going on strike, unlike their counterparts in the United States who are forbidden to do so by law. However, with the cunning of an elite group who know on which side of the bread their *beurre* is spread, the E.deF. *(Electricité de France)* struck directly at corporate France by turning the power off at 8:00 A.M., then faithfully back on every afternoon at 5:00 P.M., thus allowing the farmers to draw water from their wells and operate the milking machines morning and evening. Not a good idea to irritate the farmers, even while striking to make a point. The electrical cycle was only one among many customs to which I had to adapt.

Calvings were always exciting. I learned which cows had histories of giving birth prematurely and tried to bring any that were approaching their due dates into the barn for a little extra feed and attention and some special TLC. During these times, I spent many nights in the barn propped against a bale of fresh straw while new mamas circled and grunted. I explained breathing and relaxation techniques, but, in general, they did it all with a minimum of fuss. The new calf was a never-ending source of wonderment, both for me and its mother.

A special treat after a birth was a litre of heated wine mixed in a bucket with a cup of sugar. That was for the cow, of course, although I usually sloshed a tipple of the wine into a glass for the coach. The wine, a rasher of grain and some fresh alfalfa hay and both mama and child rested happily. By then, it was usually time for me to get up and start milking.

I have no idea what the statistics are overall for births during the day versus those at night, but I can personally attest that at *Vezat*, the majority occurred at night. I think the cows did it on purpose to be sure of my undivided attention. It was also part of the universal conspiracy to keep me from ever getting enough sleep.

One exception was Felicia, who went into labor with her first calf in the woods bordering the big field in the middle of the day.

It was a bitter cold day in February, the sky the color of old steel with the shine worn off, trees like dry sticks except for a few scrub pines and junipers which were whipping

around in the gusty winds. Felicia didn't come in with the
herd for breakfast, but I saw her grazing in the field and didn't
worry overmuch. She wasn't due for a couple of weeks yet and
I had enough to worry about with two other new mamas
learning about the milking machine, including Petula, whose
damned dragging udder became a major menace after she
calved. My legs were black and blue from some nasty kicks
during the process. That, along with some mucky tails slung
around my head and shoulders, hadn't done a lot for my disposition.

By the time I'd finished milking, gotten the kids off to
school, fed the new calves and cleaned up the labor-and-deliv-
ery barn for Felicia, it was going on noon. I grabbed a rope, a
bucket of grain—I'm not above bribery—and headed out to the
field. Felicia wasn't with the herd, but I could hear some
heavy-duty groaning just inside the woods. I walked toward
the sound and there she was, turning in circles and *meugl*-ing
in deep distress. I figured it was time I called for help.
Breathing and relaxation techniques weren't going to cut it.

Running back to the courtyard, I hopped in my car
and headed down the hill to the veterinarian's house, praying
to find him in. On the way, I crossed René on his *mobylette*
heading home for lunch and stopped briefly to share my troubles. When I got to my destination, the veterinarian, *bien sûr,*
was out, but his wife promised to send him up to our farm as
soon as he returned. *Tout de suite.* I jumped in the car and
raced back up the hill, finding both René's moped and
Gabriel's car in the courtyard and both men halfway out in
the field.

This was good news and bad news. Good news
because, at this moment, any help was better than none. Bad

because René and Gabriel had never yet, to my knowledge, exchanged a civil word between them. If one Frenchman states an opinion, a second will instinctively take an opposing view. With Gabriel and René this was a given, but the opposing view was expressed with additional comments on the intelligence level behind the opinion along with the most likely barnyard antecedents of the opinion-maker. The conversation would continue louder and more colorfully, eventually being conducted entirely in *patois*, the ancient language of the region and still much in use among the *paysans*. This way they felt I wouldn't understand and therefore both men could give free rein to the inventiveness of their vocabularies. Some things are universal.

"Mon dieu!"

"Putain!"

It was worse than I thought. Both men were staring at the hoof shoving its way out the birth passage. The calf was coming out wrong, hind feet first.

"Get a rope, Janine." Gabriel was the first to take charge.

"Gros con! You'll kill the cow." René didn't agree.

"Meuh!" Felicia was ready to settle for anything.

I stood at her head and patted her sweating neck while the men attached the rope to a small hoof. The theory was that they would pass the rope over a neighboring tree branch to obtain leverage, and pull lightly each time the cow pushed, aiding her in her endeavors. Within a few minutes, this was quite obviously not working and Felicia was showing signs of fatigue.

"This happened one time at *l'oncle's*," Gabriel said, scratching his head. "Finally had to go in and cut the calf into quarters and pull out the pieces." He nodded sagely. *"Eh oui."*

I was speechless. It's hard to talk with your jaw resting on your chest.

"Better'n losing cow and calf both, *n'est-ce pas?*" He looked to René for confirmation. "She'll still give milk. Only lose the calf."

I very nearly hugged the shy, young veterinarian, Dr. Marchaud, as he strode across the field. It's doubtful the taciturn fellow ever received such a warm welcome. Within minutes I fetched a bucket of warm soapy water and he was up to his armpits inside Felicia, turning the calf.

"It's a big 'un," he muttered, grimacing as he attempted to correct the situation.

Hard to say who labored the most: the cow, the veterinarian or the three of us, pacing and wringing our hands. Felicia lay on her side, wrung out and exhausted, when a huge wet calf popped out, bawling at its rough welcome to the world. The cow struggled to reach it, but was unable to get to her feet. The calf also lay on the ground, bawling its displeasure.

Pulling the infant around to the mother's head so she could get to the bathing process, the veterinarian palpated its hind quarters, then shook his head. *"Quel dommage!* Bet you bred her with a *Limousine* bull. Bad business, that."

I hung my head. Guilty as charged. It was common practice; breeding the cows with the larger beef bulls. This made for bigger calves, which brought more when sold. I was unaware of the risk, but ignorance has never been an acceptable excuse.

I was constantly amazed when the "dirty old man with the long arm" (the cow inseminator) surveyed his group of test tubes and related the breeds and pedigrees of the bulls represented while asking which I preferred for the cow of the moment. It was surprising to me that he didn't bring photos to show the ladies. Seems like they should have had some choice in the matter.

Dr. Marchaud dried his arms and gathered up his tools. He explained that both the cow and her calf were paralyzed in their hindquarters from the heavy pressure during the birthing. "It will clear itself up within a week or two," he said then paused. "Or it won't. Only time will tell." In the meantime, Felicia would need to be milked and her calf would need the nourishment.

"Bonne chance," he called cheerily as he headed back to his car.

Good luck, indeed!

While we loaded the crippled calf into the back of my Renault 4-L, the leaden sky leaked a fine icy mist, covering an unhappy new mama who was unable to rise to her feet and trot after her baby. We settled the baby in fresh, dry straw in the barn. Afterward, René and Gabriel left to attend to their own chores and I carried a bucket of warm, sweetened wine out to Felicia along with a hearty serving of grain.

I was already late picking up the kids at school, the cows were gathering at the gate bellowing for attention, the chickens were squawking in the courtyard and every dog and cat in the place was underfoot. And soggy.

Now was the time, I decided, as the children got into the car and we drove back to the farm, to take the boys up on their offer to milk the cows while I did "other stuff." They came through like troopers. Morning and evening we milked Felicia lying down in the field. The boys took turns—they milked the top two *tetines* while I talked to Felicia and held her to keep her quiet, then we grabbed her thrashing legs, flopped her over on her opposite side and they took care of the other two.

The mist turned into steady rains, drenching the trees, the field and the prone cow. We rigged a lean-to over her and brought her fresh alfalfa hay and buckets of grain, along with a daily bucket of sweet wine. She was wet and supine, but happy. Every morning after the rains started, Felicia would slide down the slick field in a trail of soggy grass, mud and *merde* and every evening we re-built the rickety lean-to over the cow and her evening meal.

Nourishment is very important in the beginning of a calf's life. A newborn calf needs its mother's milk for the first five days, I was instructed. This fills its need for those special nutrients. Five days was also the amount of time after the cow gave birth required by the dairy company before they would accept that cow's milk. *An interesting example of congruity*, I thought.

Our little calf quickly learned to drink his milk from a bucket. I lured his head in with a rubber nipple and he was soon sucking up large quantities of the warm nourishing fluid. He scrabbled around piteously in the fresh straw and it required a firm hand to keep the bucket upright.

When I arrived with his milk on the fifth morning, I found him standing. His front and rear ends moved in different directions as if receiving reverse instructions. But he was up, bouncy and hungry.

Three days later Felicia scrambled upright when I brought her evening libation. To my sons' great joy, I led her into the barn for milking. I think Felicia preferred it, too.

The young veterinarian passed by a day or so later to see how Felicia and her calf were doing. He told me that a neighbor up the hill had a cow with a similar problem who was kept in the barn. She had contracted an infection and died within the week. We had been most fortunate, he said, and I agreed.

As the winter months passed, the rains drizzled to an end, the sun returned and I removed the lean-to and raked the remnants of hay off the field. Felicia returned to the barn early every evening, searching through her dinner rations and regarding me with a quizzical eye. I'm sure she felt that wine with dinner was a most civilized custom and could not understand why it was not forthcoming every night.

❧ CHAPTER 22 ❧

Life, Death and Returning Seasons

A s we came to know the village of Saint-Cyprien and visited other villages traveling throughout the Dordogne, the only churches we ever laid eyes on were Catholic. These beautiful stone churches had been here for centuries. Seeing them always sparked my speculation on the lives of the men and women who had worshipped in them in ages past.

It was therefore a thrill to anticipate the arrival of that most Christian of holidays, Easter, which the French called *Pâques*. Actually, in our village I knew very few men who went to church on a regular basis. Baptisms were big events, weddings and, of course, funerals. While the ladies of the village attended church on Sunday mornings, their menfolk were in the local *taverne* placing their bets on the *tiercé*, the trotting races, and joining in a *pastis*, a syrupy, anise-flavored liqueur.

In general, other than picking up a warm, crusty loaf from the *boulangerie* and perhaps a fresh *tarte aux pommes* or *éclairs aux chocolat* as a special treat for dinner, Sundays were much like any other day for me. I stuck to worshipping in the natural beauty of my hilltop.

However, on Ash Wednesday, I noticed that Gabriel had a fresh rubbing of ashes on his forehead and a tiny palm pinned to his shirt.

"So, Gabriel, what are you giving up for Lent?" I asked.

"*Moi?*" He chuckled. "I'm going to give up water for Lent and drink only wine. *Après tout*, isn't that what the Good Lord drank?" Frankly, I'd never seen a drop of water pass his lips.

"Gabriel, were you baptized in the church?" I asked.

"*Mais, bien sûr!*" he responded.

"And were you married in the church?" I asked.

"*Bien sûr que oui!*" he answered.

"And will your funeral be in the church?" I continued.

"Not soon, I hope, *mais absolument.*"

"Gabriel, you make fun of the church, you insist you don't believe in many of its teachings and yet for every major occasion, there you are. It doesn't make sense."

Gabriel laughed heartily and slapped his thigh. "It just doesn't pay to take chances. *On sait jamais!*"

One never knows. My thoughts echoed his words.

The Lenten season, in a farming community, is a time of re-birth. The grasses in the fields turn deeper green and imperceptibly thicken and push upwards. Seeds planted in tilled land emerge as tiny sprouts. Trees, barren at night, awaken in the morning, newly covered in leafy robes. It happens silently with no fanfare, no trumpets, only the birds singing in the trees, yellow chicks hatching and fresh, vernal new growth everywhere. Flowers appear at the monthly fair, their brilliant colors of red, blue and yellow bringing brightness to the still grey skies.

The cherry tree down by the spring bursts into masses of blooms, promising a plentiful crop. I watched the tree carefully each spring as the tiny fruit replaced the blossoms, growing plump and juicy and changing slowly from green to red. I never tasted a single cherry. Flocks of birds also watched carefully and never failed to beat me to the harvest, cleaning the tree like a horde of pickers being paid by the piece. Each year I plotted to pick the cherries just a bit earlier, even if not quite ripe, and each year the birds were a day ahead of me. It seemed unnecessarily spiteful of them to drop the pits in the courtyard as they flew overhead.

During Holy Week, the village stores changed their window decorations, adding bright touches of color and the *patissiere* added baskets filled with colored eggs and tiny cakes with bright frosting.

I missed the chocolate bunnies, as did the children. The Easter Bunny simply did not exist here. Chicks and eggs, yes, in abundance, but no hopping bunny hiding eggs in the dark of night.

Then, as the Easter season progressed, I discovered something entirely new in my experience, which captured my taste buds. *Pain de Pâques*, Easter bread. I became utterly addicted to it. The bread was only available Easter week and then only in limited quantities. *Pain de Pâques* was round and soft, lightly flavored with anise. Under normal circumstances, I stay as far as possible away from licorice and anything with licorice flavoring, but *pain de Pâques* had a very delicate anise flavor, blended with other spices and lightly sweetened. I could eat an entire loaf in one sitting. There is absolutely no doubt that if it had been available more often or in larger quantities, I would have gained three hundred pounds and become a total slave to that golden loaf.

Each spring, I started watching the *boulangerie* closely a few weeks before Easter. When questioned, the *boulangère* would shake her head, smile and say, *"Ah oui, bientôt, un de ces jours,"*—soon, one of these days—leaving me to continually haunt the premises. Then the bread would appear magically one morning and be gone by nightfall, not to reappear until the following year.

In this small, relatively poor, rural village in France, we found that Easter and other holidays did not hold the same commercial overtones we'd known in the States. Holidays in Saint-Cyprien focused on their original meanings and were celebrated always with family and close friends. *Pâques* was an opportunity for a magnificent feast with a special pastry and a special time to give thanks. Thanks for new births among the beasts, new growth in the fields and for the renewed promise of His eternal love.

It was not long after *Pâques* that I sat beneath the oak tree one night, musing on the meaning of past, present and future and on the meaning of things both personal and profound. In the dark night, I became conscious of the planets conducting their measured dance, a stately push and pull, continually responding to an internal music not quite heard, but felt through the rhythm, the breathy response of our own planet. I pondered, along with the life around me—the owls who-o-ing softly, the oak leaves whispering—the usual rush of personal insignificance within the mystery of vast endlessness. Deep metaphysical truths rattled around in my skull and I waited for the presence of God.

And waited. This particular night, my eyes felt burned dry and my head throbbed from a day spent cradling a young sheep through the torment of her dying. I couldn't help, although heaven knows, I tried.

Returning to the farm after dropping the kids at school, I gathered tools in preparation for a few hours of fence repair. When all other chores pall, there's always that. Heading out through the back field, I heard Babette *bell*-ing. As French cows do not moo, but *meugle*, French sheep don't baaa, they *bell*.

Most farms don't mix cows and sheep, but after having adopted several orphaned lambs and creating spoiled adolescents, I couldn't simply turn them out into the world. Therefore, we built a small enclosure on the hillside, with grass for grazing and a few trees for shade. The clothesline was also there for the simple reason that there was nowhere else to put it.

Babette wasn't *bell*-ing for attention, however, it was a cry of sheer distress. She was running in short hops, circling, her belly bloated as if she were producing quadruplets. She wasn't pregnant. She was barely old enough to create a spark of interest in the eye of a *belier*, a ram. I opened the gate, pushed the other woolly bodies back and drew her out and down the hill into the courtyard. We went into one of the stables, cool and smelling of fresh straw mixed with leftover baby calf fragrance from the last occupant.

She circled in distress, moaned, lay down, stood up and head butted my legs for comfort. She'd been born a twin, found in a neighbor's stable in the morning, mom and sister dead, herself butted mercilessly by the herd as she sought breakfast. We'd adopted her (our reputation as suckers for orphans was spreading), bottle fed her every four hours, day and night, snuggled her warmly in a towel-lined box near the heater in the kitchen. She had a sweet nature and an unbelievable greediness for anything edible, as if in memory of the morning after her birth. Anything was grist for her maw: the children's books and homework, chair cushions, her own box. Dogs and cats zealously defended their bowls, leaving nothing for the bouncy lamb.

Eventually, as she grew into a young *brebis*, she was evicted from the kitchen and joined our small herd of orphans. I often allowed her to join the troupe of beasts that followed me on my regular tours of the fence line. Gabriel entered the courtyard one day and was struck speechless as he watched me returning from the fields followed by two dogs, three cats, a turkey, two guinea hens and Babette. He shook his head, chortling, and declared that called for a glass of wine. What didn't?

I filled a bucket of water and left it in the stable for Babette, while I ran for the car and roared down the hill to Dr. Marchaud, the kindly veterinarian.

"Mais, Madame, il est parti. Les vaccins, vous savez. Six heures. Il sera là a six heures." Gone. I'd forgotten it was the time of year for vaccinating cows. He'd be back at six this evening.

I got back in the car and circled the village, the side roads, everywhere, looking for René on his postal route. When I found him, he smiled merrily, then caught sight of my face.

"Qu'est-ce que c'est, Janine? Les enfants sont malade?" No, the children were fine, but it was one of my babies, nevertheless.

I explained and he nodded. *"Eh oui, ça arrive."* That happens. Eating too fast, too much, the heat, any number of reasons for the bloat. No, not much to do. The gas must escape. Perhaps a hole in the stomach? The vet was out? Ah, well, it didn't often work anyway. She would live or she would die.

"Mais, elle souffre, René." She's suffering, I sobbed.

"Alors, il faut couper la gorge," Cut her throat!

"Pas possible!" I said shaking my head.

He patted my hand, assured me that he would stop by after he finished his route. It was good I'd brought her in. The barn would be cooler, more comfortable. With the ease of generations of farmers, he accepted the unacceptable. He found no reason to question why. The cause of death was inevitably life.

I returned home and quietly slipped into the stable. She was lying on her side now, breathing in short gasps, the obscenely bloated stomach rising like a beach ball behind the suffering eyes. I sat, pulling the soft head onto my lap. I told her it was her own fault, her greed finally did her in. My tears fell on the matted wool. We stayed there most of the afternoon, until she lay still and cold.

That night I watched the dance of the planets, the inevitable ponderous motions of eternity. And wondered why.

An unusually warm summer quickly passed and I found myself, come fall, still pondering the strange juxtapositions of life and death, joy and sorrow, remembering and forgetting.

The leaves performed their autumnal ritual, changing themselves magically into vivid orange, red and yellow spectacles, then fluttering to the ground one by one. Small birds and animals rooted amongst them for one last acorn, the cows and deer nuzzled deeper seeking errant blades of grass. The winds playfully tossed them into piles, banking them against aged stumps and hillocks. Then, beaten by the rain into a sodden carpet, I saw that they'd spread throughout the woods to nurture and provide color inspiration to the forest mushrooms, the tall, elongated *morilles* and the wide, flat *cèpes*, perhaps even some deadly, orange *amanite tue-mouches*.

The farmers had completed the year's harvests and were spreading walnuts in attics and on racks to dry. The fields had been plowed for the winter's repose, the earth turned and waiting for nutrients to fall from the sky. The hogs were in final countdown before slaughter.

Gabriel had suggested many times that I really ought to raise a pig. How he thought I could take one of those cute, little, soft, pink creatures, feed it twice daily, watch it grow fat and sassy, coming when I called it by name, then hoist it up by its dainty hind hoofs and slit its throat, was beyond me.

My boys, however, found the process fascinating. Danny was the first to participate in the annual event. He'd spent a Saturday with a friend from a farm on the other side of the village.

"How was your day? Have fun?" I inquired, as he hopped off his bicycle in the courtyard in the late afternoon.

"Man! It was great!" He could hardly contain himself. "I helped slaughter the hog." As I stood in dumfounded silence at this evidence of basic bloodthirstiness, he recounted the details of the gory event.

During this season of the year, I exercised caution in whom I visited. I had a deep aversion to seeing Pompidou, DeGaulle, Charles, Louis or Napoleon strung up by his heels dripping his lifeblood into buckets. This was one project my friends and neighbors could do without my help.

The slaughter occupied all the men of the household, fulfilling their roles as providers for the family. This was a testosterone-driven event. The days following were ones of intense activity for the women, cooking and preserving every usable portion of the pig for the winter to come.

Freezers, for small provincial farmers, were still an unknown and untested product. Certainly, no French farm wife worth her pâté would risk a year's supply of meat to such a newfangled invention. And that was without even taking into account the regular occurrences of strikes, storms and other interruptions to the electric service. Therefore, the pork required cooking and canning, the time-tested methods of preservation.

For the next few days after the butchering, kettles constantly simmered with chunks of pork in the preparation of *confits de porc, grillons de porc, pâté de campagne,* as well as in rendering the pots of lard which would serve as cooking grease for the following year. My guess is that, at the end of the week, the majority of the *bonnes femmes* didn't care if they ever saw another piece of pork again as long as they lived. But the storage shelves were filled with gleaming jars of preserved meat, enough to last a long, cold winter.

René and Jane didn't raise their own pig, but René joined in the fever by visiting the *abbatoire* to select a choice leg, which treasure he carried home to rub with his special blend of garlic and spices, then tenderly placed in a wooden box built exactly to fit the ham with just sufficient space for a goodly snug of rock salt. Over the next month or two, he checked the box from time to time to adjust the salt, making sure no pink skin was uncovered. When the *jambon de pays* was removed from the box, it was placed in a cloth bag and hung in royal state from a hook on a beam in the kitchen-dining-living room. He had only disdain for the *pauvres cons* who hung their hams uncovered, thus allowing resting places for passing flies.

Special dinners involved the ham being lifted down with reverence and paper thin slices placed on each plate to be eaten with morsels of melon or perhaps a crusty chunk of bread spread thinly with sweet butter. A family meal might include a thicker slice, fried lightly with an egg or served with vegetables and a *bonnè sauce roux*. Finally, of course, the *pièce de resistance* was achieved when the bone was placed in the cookpot with a head of cabbage and a few carrots for *la soupe*.

The closest I have come to the flavor of the *jambon de pays* since my time in France, is tasting a good prosciutto. I believe its true essence, however, lies in the ambiance, the expectant hush while the ham is sliced or maybe it's all a matter of attitude, which René had in abundance.

No part of the hog, however small or unimportant, was wasted. The blood was gathered in buckets and mixed with a small amount of vinegar to prevent coagulation (heaven forbid! like lumps in the oatmeal) and the intestines were thoroughly washed in preparation for *les boudins*, the blood sausage. This sausage, beloved of the locals, was prepared by secret family recipes, including combinations of morsels of neck, head and other bits and pieces which are best not discussed in detail, simmered together with spices and seasonings, then added to chunks of lard, the whole concoction mixed up with the blood and stuffed into the intestines. These sausages were tied off with string at foot-long intervals and presented to dear friends and passersby during the following week.

I learned to avoid visiting pig-raising friends during this time or even driving near their farms, since they were known to run out to the road waving strings of *boudin,* a hospitable gesture and impossible to refuse.

We tried cooking up the sausage for dinner, but the entire family, with the exception of Tim and the dogs, all of whom loved the stuff, decided the time was appropriate to open the latest jar of peanut butter sent by Aunt Pat.

Economics 101

After a while, it began to look as if my current career choice would, just barely, cover basic living needs. Food. Utilities. Gas for the car and tractor. Just the basics. The cows were doing their best, but, let's face it, milk isn't diamonds or even truffles. It's milk. And while it always ranked right up there in the butterfat percentages for the highest pay scale, the girls could only produce so much.

In order to provide an income source to cover purchases of fertilizer, clothes, veterinarian bills and other necessities of life, I raised baby calves up to large adult cows for sale to other dairy farmers. My ladies often provided the infant stock for this free of charge or thereabouts. However, they also often produced male calves which weren't what I wanted (How many bulls does one farm need, anyway?) and I needed a larger number of female calves than I could reasonably expect from my own herd. Therefore, I was stuck with buying calves from neighboring farms or from the livestock merchants.

There we were, face to face with one of the basic precepts of any economics class—it takes money to make money. I needed cash to buy the calves and feed them, then let the money float for a year to eighteen months before selling the animals and recouping the original investment plus, one hoped, a sizeable profit. For my neighbors, it was money from the tobacco crop which provided this financial float. For me, it was my friendly banker.

My credit at the local *Credit Agricole*, was pretty good. We had purchased an excellent farm property for cash; it was well stocked with beasts and was being farmed (they had absolutely no idea of my skill or lack thereof). As far as they knew, my husband was still actively involved although largely absentee and there were still dollars being deposited into my account from time to time (the irregularity and ever diminishing amounts hadn't yet rung any bells). Therefore, when I presented my request for a loan to cover the purchase of several calves, it was considered briefly and granted. I couldn't believe my luck. On the other hand, I really think the banker wondered privately why Americans (everyone knows how rich they are) needed to borrow this piddling sum. Little did he know!

Anyway, my calves thrived on three months of twice-daily buckets of milk made from mixing warm water with dry milk powder from the farm co-op plus cracked corn or barley and alfalfa all grown on the farm, then several months of grazing in fertile fields augmented by more grains. When we sold them a year later, they were sleek and chubby, ready to be bred and join a milking herd. They were also gentle and thoroughly domesticated (practically house pets) and their new owners, sent to me by my friends and neighbors, were ecstatic. By the following year, our reputation was made.

Financially, we did well on the *elevage du veaux*, raising calves, but, quite frankly, I never knew where I stood.
After selling the last calf, I paid off the bank then made the
rounds paying bills for tractor parts and repairs, vet bills, co-
op bills, buying fertilizer and seed for the fields and new
shoes for the kids along with a few pairs of jeans and
sweaters, with never quite enough left over to purchase
another set of calves and there I was, back at the bank. The
prices for buying calves and selling cows fluctuated with the
same constancy as the commodities market on the New York
Stock Exchange and the same guidelines prevailed—buy low,
sell high. I was constantly teetering on a high wire without
the comfort of knowing a net was firmly in place below.

Then I decided I needed a new milking barn down
below the big hay barn, which would keep the cows from
tromping through the courtyard twice daily and assuring that
anyone walking to or from our front door had to pass through
quantities of mud and muck. I didn't want anything fancy, not
even a closed in structure, but rather an *appenti*, a lean-to
consisting of a roof and a wall on the east side to break the
wind, leaving the south and west open. It would provide shelter, be readily accessible for the cows and there'd even be
space for a milk cooler to keep the *bidons* cool until I could
deliver them to the Rougier farm for pick-up. Then, I could
have the courtyard blacktopped. Such luxury. Such expense!

On top of everything else, the French postal service
was on an extended strike which involved the sorting facilities in Paris refusing to do their job of distributing the mail
entering the country. Pictures on the television showed bags
of international mail piled bag upon bag upon bag in huge
warehouses. This meant that absolutely no dollars, not even

diminishing ones, were arriving. *Okay*, I thought, *I'm going to have to get creative.*

All of this was happening at the same time as one of the cyclic shortages of gas and oil in France. Rationing at the local gas station was severe and rigidly enforced, although we were fortunate since farmers were exempt. Farms, after all, were the basis of the local economy and must be allowed to function. Oil for heating systems was also severely rationed and complaints were resounding all over the country with heavy winter snows predicted and a chilly fall already well in progress. This, incidentally, didn't concern us since we had no heating system.

Consequently, wood for heating purposes was at a premium. And *Vezat* was blessed with more than a third of its fifty acres full to overflowing with juniper, pine, oak, birch; big trees, little trees, medium-sized trees. The father of one of Wendy's friends was a wood cutter for a major dealer in wood and he arranged for his boss to come by and give me a quote on cutting down just enough trees to clear out old growth and open up a few pastures. The dealer was thrilled, the friend's father was excited to have a job so close to home and I was ecstatic with the price offered.

For the next month the sounds of a power saw zapped the stillness of the countryside from early morning to late afternoon. Most of the wood cutting was being done in the woods around the farthest outlying fields and I often wandered back to watch Jean-Jacques cut. Different trees were cut for different uses; tall oaks were cut in six- and nine-foot lengths for use as mine posts, birch trees were cut up to be used in the paper mills and others were chopped into even smaller lengths for firewood. Jean-Jacques piled all of these at the edge of the field, neatly sorted by size and intended use, and it was my job to transport them to a spot alongside our lane where the heavy-duty transport trucks would pick them up. If the wood merchant was obliged to send smaller trucks out to pick up the wood in the fields, my check would have been cut by nearly half.

For the next few weeks, my sons and I earned every roof tile, beam and block in our new barn. Every afternoon after school we headed to the back field with the tractor and *remorque*. We'd have just enough time to bring in one big load before milking, homework and dinner. Saturdays and Sundays became full work days, starting immediately after milking, hauling load after load until nearly dark, then milking again, homework and supper. The girls helped too, with Wendy doing most of the supper cooking and Jill taking care of the rabbits, chickens and other miscellany. You might say this was a team effort.

We had high hopes that the two-week Christmas break would see the end of the job. However, every element fought us, from bitter cold with snow flurries to drizzly rains to thaws created by the afternoon sun that created rivers of mud under the tractor wheels. The tractor itself wasn't too cooperative about rising and shining in the frigid early hours. Its parts were plumb frozen solid, I guess. So we took to parking it on the hill behind the house where we could release the brake, give it a mighty shove and start it gasping by the time it reached the courtyard. We also had some magic spray which, we were told, should be sprayed into the exhaust pipe. This spray worked wonders. I wished I could find one for human consumption.

We dressed in about fifty layers of clothing and wore boots with multiple socks on our feet. We still got cold. But it was our hands that suffered the most. The first load of the morning, before any ray of sun had reached the woods, was the worst. The woodpiles were covered with a light film of snow and each piece was frozen solid to the ones around it. We tried tugging, then kicking them and finally settled on carrying a large wrench on the tractor for the sole purpose of whacking those blocks apart.

Every lesson there was to be learned about hauling wood, we learned. Unfortunately, we learned most of them the hard way. If the trailer was loaded too high, the nose of the tractor would just lift itself straight up in the air, wheels spinning futilely. One of us had to drive the tractor and the other two would leap up and hang on the front end, but even that wasn't always enough and we'd have to toss off some of the already-loaded logs. Then we learned about weights made especially for this purpose which fit into a frame on the front end of the tractor. Even with the weights, we still often needed to ride the front of the tractor over low hills. That was the only time in my life I ever wished I weighed more than I actually did.

By the time we made the final run of the day one bright sunny afternoon, the coating of snow and frost had melted and the passages of the tractor and heavily-weighted trailer had created a viscous mudhole at the courtyard entry. The cows' water *bac* was also located nearby and the girls' traffic to and fro hadn't helped the situation any. We were getting near the end of our task and had piled the wood especially high. Tim was at the wheel of the tractor, I walked alongside and Dan went ahead to open the gate. Suddenly, as the wheels slithered and spun in the mud, the trailer hitch pivoted. Then the entire load of logs tipped over, pouring down into the woods and field below.

Dan and Tim surveyed the situation with horror. I cried. As the boys headed down to start the retrieval process, I called them back.

"No way, guys. It's too late tonight. It'll be our first load in the morning."

After a weary Christmas day, I gave them another day off during the holiday school break. Those kids had worked like men, more than that, like supermen. I planned to take care of other chores that day, too, but Jean-Jacques said he'd come up and give me a hand if I wanted to bring in another load or two of wood. It was the second load and we were working on a pile of six-footers. I took the front end of a log, Jean-Jacques had the rear and we swung it up onto the *remorque*. Only my hand slipped and the weight of the post pushed the back of my hand into and through the bare metal wheel-cover on the trailer. At first, I thought it was okay, just a bump. Then the blood starting gushing through my mitten and the numbness was replaced with pulsating pain.

Jean-Jacques stared at me, turning greenish white. I thought he was going to throw up.

"*Qu'est-ce qu'on fait?*" He was asking *me* what to do?

I pulled off the mitten and peered at my hand. The ring finger of my right hand was covered in blood and gleamed white beneath. The metal had cut through to the bone.

"Can you drive me to Dr. DeJean's?" I asked.

"I guess," but he didn't look at all sure.

He started back to the house on foot, but I suggested we take the tractor. It'd be faster in the long run. Jean-Jacques drove the tractor into the courtyard, but I got off and wound up driving the car to town, because he was trembling too much.

"Nom de Dieu!" he kept murmuring, shaking his head.

Dr. DeJean put in several stitches. Then he wrapped my hand with a huge bandage, gave me a couple of shots and some pills for pain. He had Jean-Jacques lie down with cold cloths on his head while he worked on me. Jean-Jacques got the sympathy and Tender, Loving Care and I received the medical skills. I guess that was for the best, but I felt that it wasn't really fair.

The boys and I finished the wood job the first weekend after the new year, just as the Paris postal workers settled their strike. That last load seemed to take forever. We were so slaphappy with exhaustion and relief that we giggled our way through flinging the final log onto the pile.

The boys definitely earned a major reward. Mine was the new milking barn. One of the unplanned benefits was the ringside seat I was given for each succeeding sunrise as tentative fingers of light moved across the hillside until the sun popped above the river. In the evenings, I had a view of changing colors across the hills and sky, from amber through mauve to rose to a deep cerulean blue. Often I caught twinkles from the first stars.

As I contemplated the natural beauty of the Dordogne, I counted my many blessings. A mud- and dung-free courtyard ranked high on the list.

❧ CHAPTER 24 ❧

Thanksgiving

It took us several years of learning new customs before we realized a major holiday was missing from our lives. I guess the French forefathers never felt the need to gather with the Gauls and give thanks while roasting whole, stuffed turkeys and cooking up corn bread and pumpkin pie. The children and I decided to have our own Thanksgiving celebration, but all we could find at the local *boucherie* was chicken. Somehow, *coq au vin*, French bread and *eclair au chocolat*, while tasty, just wasn't right for a Thanksgiving feast. We were told, with unnecessary acidity, I thought, that if we wanted to roast a turkey we should raise it ourselves. We had a farm, for heaven's sake!

That November was lost to us, but we vowed to start planning for the next year. In early spring, at the monthly street fair where the farmers were selling infant poultry, we bought two young turkey chicks. I swore that I was going to be a practical farmer and raise them to eat. These turkeys would NOT become pets. I promptly named them Pauline and Petunia.

Petunia seemed a reasonable name, even cute, when he was a fluffy yellow chick of undetermined sex living in a cardboard box warmed by a forty watt light bulb. It was still okay as he grew into a gangly adolescent trotting after me as if I were his mom. But when he grew into a big, black, ugly tom with a flabby red flap hanging down the side of his head and under his chin, his name was just plain dumb.

Pauline became a beautiful, gentle, white hen. We would never have considered having her grace a festive Thanksgiving table, browned and stuffed with drumsticks pointing skyward.

Petunia worshipped me, don't ask me why. He certainly had no inkling of the fate planned for him. He followed me wherever possible, came when I called him and even nudged caressingly around my legs, like the dogs or cats. He loathed everyone else, however, particularly anyone who approached me. When friends dropped by and attempted to shake my hand, he flew into a rage, his head changing from red through shades of purple to blue, the black tail feathers fanning out as he flew at the visitor, flapping his great wings and pecking his ugly beak at a leg, an arm or a foot.

He lurked at the end of the lane for the children to return home from school on their bicycles and *mobylettes* and greeted them with squawks and flying talons. They roared into the courtyard with their feet up on the handlebars and flailed their bookbags at the furious bird, simultaneously yelling, "Mom, call off your mangy critter!" They counted the days to Thanksgiving and, once safely at the door called back to him, "Just you wait, you ugly bird, just you wait!"

One day two American ladies living in a nearby village, having heard of the rare presence of other Americans in the area, decided to pay us a visit. The elderly widow and her divorced, thirtyish daughter, living off investment income and alimony, called themselves writers and enjoyed the company of the mainly English literary expatriate community. (The area has been home to many English people, dating back to the twelfth century, when Eleanor of Aquitaine married the heir to the throne of England. It remained English until the fifteenth century, when it was annexed by France at the end of the Hundred Years' War.)

No doubt the ladies anticipated finding a family of Americans playing at farming while enjoying the cultural experience of rural France. Our three-hundred-year-old semi ruin must have come as a bit of a shock, but it was Petunia who made the greatest impression on their sheltered lives.

The afternoon of the visit, of which we were totally unaware, was the day we took our annual clothes shopping expedition to Sarlat and we were away until nearly dusk. The ladies arrived mid-afternoon and parked just outside the central court, but as they opened the car doors to get out they were greeted by a furious black turkey, squawking and seeming to fly at both doors simultaneously. Startled, they jumped back inside and slammed the doors. For the next couple of hours they watched from inside the car as he did his strange dance around them, like a Mexican hat dance with the car as the crown of the hat. Back and forth, tail feathers spread peacock-style, he strutted and hopped, performing his version of the turkey trot. They could have driven out at any time, but as they related to us later, they were so enchanted by his antics, they were loath to leave and sat for hours in fascinated wonderment until we returned.

By the time mid-November rolled around, I was less and less interested in cooking a Thanksgiving turkey, certainly not one of my own babies, even if one of them was aggressive and slightly deranged. The children were considerably less sentimental and relished their mental image of a plucked Petunia lying fragrant and steaming on a platter. They reminded me of our status as farmers and my vow to be practical. They reiterated our need to eat what we raised and emphasized their total lack of desire to become vegetarians.

Finally, driven to the wall, I conceded, but agreed to do the cooking only if they would do the slaughtering and the plucking. From the lights in my sons' eyes, I could see that this was not a hardship, but more of a reward and a true reason for giving thanks.

The morning of the Great Murder, the girls and I decided on an expedition to the village. Actually, only Jill, the youngest, had originally planned to accompany me away from the scene of the crime—until the boys started sharpening tools and planning strategy. Wendy had looked forward to the event almost as ghoulishly as her brothers, but, at the last minute, turned pea-green and decided that perhaps, after all, she did need a book from the *librairie*. Taking one last look at my black-feathered chick who was at the moment scarfing down all the chicken feed while vociferously threatening any of the other poultry who dared approach, the girls and I left the boys to their macabre deed.

An hour later when we could think of no other possible errand in the village, we started back up the hill. With trepidation we approached the courtyard, but could see no evidence of the massacre other than a black feather or two. We walked into the kitchen, where Danny and Tim were devouring chunks of bread and hot chocolate as their treat for a job well done.

"Man, that bird's head turned every color of the rainbow!"

"We had to chase him all around the cornfield AFTER chopping off his head. Talk about yucky!"

Dan laughed so hard he snorted chocolate and Tim was pounding his knees.

"We finally strung him up by the feet to let him drain and hung him on the trailer hitch on the hay wagon."

"Didn't you see him, Mom, as you drove in?"

Stomachs churning, we looked blank. There'd been nothing on the hay trailer as we came in. Was he once again up and running around, our very own headless turkey?

"Did the dogs take him?"

"No, the dogs are right here!" Danny pointed to the dogs flopped under the table, noses poised for a crumb to drop.

"Well, what? How? Why?"

Questions flew, but no answers. We walked into the courtyard and over to the hay trailer. No turkey. Suddenly, Gabriel popped out from behind it, his puckish face split into a wide grin. We should have known. Laughing so hard as to be nearly incoherent, he pointed down into the nearby woods. We ran down and nearly collided with Petunia strung up on an oak branch.

"*Quelle blague!* What a joke! Those worried faces! Did you think your headless turkey had run away?" And he was off in another paroxysm of laughter.

The Thanksgiving dinner was pronounced a great success. We all gave thanks for each other, for the bounty of the

food and of our lives. My "rotten" kids gave thanks that
Petunia was finally serving a useful purpose. I privately gave
thanks for my my "rotton" kids, my best beloveds, the joy and
reason for my very existence. And for friends and for laughter.

I ate a vegetarian meal.

CHAPTER 25

Good-byes and Hellos

Just as one animal crisis faded, another one erupted, a situation that seemed to be a constant in our lives.

"Mom, he's having a fit. You gotta come. NOW!" Tim's voice squeaked in desperation.

I sat back on the little three-legged stool and wiped the back of my arm across my sweaty forehead—right in the middle of milking and another emergency. "Who's having a fit?" I called through the empty doorway.

"It's Schultz, Mom. He can't breathe. You gotta do something. PLEASE!" Both tears and panic were in Tim's voice as the milking machine pulled the last drops from Lily and I disconnected. Running outside the barn, I found Schultz, our sturdy little dachshund, writhing on the ground. Picking him up, I raced for the car, Tim at my heels.

"Danny, please finish the milking. There's only Petula left," I hollered into the air, praying that my other son would hear. Jumping into the car, I slammed it into gear and we tore out the gravel road.

Dr. Marchaud was barely a mile away, but the little dog had ceased gasping and lay still in Tim's arms by the time we pulled up to the veterinarian's door. The stocky young man looked at our tear-streaked faces with compassion and tenderly placed Schultz on his examining table, shaking his head.

Peering into the dog's long slender muzzle, he said, "Well, here it is. He's been stung in the throat by a wasp. The swelling blocked the airway." The vet had covered miles that day seeing cattle, sheep, horses, even rabbits afflicted by a terrible epidemic. But his tired brown eyes were filled with sympathy. "There was nothing you could have done."

We had hoped for a miracle and it didn't happen. Our friend was dead. The laughing dog had snapped at his last bug. Now the chickens' tail feathers could grow without risk. But our little family was devastated.

Penny, the black Labrador, searched everywhere for her pal and constant companion and sprawled listlessly in the courtyard, muzzle on paws, while the chickens pecked around her for seed. A rather small dog had left a huge, gaping hole in all our lives.

It was a couple of months later, one quiet afternoon when the children were in school, that Gabriel's old car rattled down the lane.

"*Allez-y*," he called, "come for a ride. I've got something to show you. Don't worry, we'll be back before school's out."

Try as I might, I couldn't wheedle from him our destination. Gabriel just chuckled, eyes dancing with mischief. We pulled into the lane of a rundown farm with fences sagging more precipitously than his ever did, rotting straw and manure piled in the courtyard. The stench was unbelievable. I gagged and eyed Gabriel with distrust. What the hell was he getting me in to now?

I could never determine the ages of many of the local farmers. With their dusty berets, blue coveralls and weathered skin, they could be thirty or eighty. The one approaching us had recently been close to a bottle of wine, but was a stranger to soap and water. He greeted Gabriel with the bonhomie of a used car salesman and leered at me. Dogs barked and bayed in the background, covering the introductions, and Gabriel grabbed his arm before he could shake my hand, leading him toward the pens.

Never have I seen so many dogs of so many different breeds. Nor have I ever seen dogs of such thinness, with ribs sticking out like xylophone keys. Our host yelled something incomprehensible and the din ceased, instantly. This was a doggy hell and Beelzebub had spoken. As a matter of fact, should one of these animals have the good fortune to die and descend to the Nether Regions, it would be a distinct step up from its current residence. The dog at his side walked warily, tail firmly tucked under his belly, fearful eyes never leaving his master.

I had grown used to the smell of a clean farm, that mix of dried alfalfa, fresh grass, *parfum de* cow and, even, *eau de* cow manure. It's a smell of promise, of life and hope, cycles and seasons. But this was different. This was rotten and stale. The dogs were imprisoned in the filthiest pens I had ever laid eyes on. Their eyes spoke what I couldn't bear to hear. I looked at Gabriel in shock that he would bring me here, but he shushed me. I couldn't believe that he, Gabriel, who loved all beasts, would even know such a man.

We walked toward a smaller pen, containing a bitch with five puppies, a small dachshund and five tiny Schultzes. I forgot the awful surroundings and stepped forward with delight, but Gabriel put his hand quietly on my arm and shook his head. *"Taisez-vous.* Let me do the talking," he muttered in an aside as the farmer entered the pen.

Suddenly, I noticed with horror the little mother flinching as the farmer approached her, but he simply grabbed one of the pups and handed it out to us. He praised the breeding stock, as I held the tiny creature. She was thin, but from the state of the mother, it was amazing that she was alive at all. The farmer explained that she was four weeks old and was the only one not promised. These undernourished little animals were, in his eyes, "prime hunting stock."

I held the trembling puppy up to my face, cooing, and a pink tongue reached out to rasp across my cheek. That did it! I was lost. Before I knew what was going on, Gabriel was bargaining. At one point he leaned over to me and asked if I could afford 5,000 francs. 5,000 francs! My God, that was $1,000! *No, wait,* I thought. *That wasn't right.*

Right after World War II in an attempt to stabilize a disastrous economy, the government of France devalued the franc by 100:1. The *paysans* still spoke in *anciens francs.* The first time I was charged *cent francs* (100 francs) for a loaf of bread I nearly had a heart attack.

This habit of talking in 'old' francs still caused me heart palpitations, but as I calculated backwards, it became fifty "new" francs or ten dollars. I nodded and Gabriel reached out his hand for a contractual handshake. I grubbed in my purse for the bills and we were in the car, the puppy still quivering in my hands.

"But, Gabriel, she's too young to leave her mother," I protested as his ancient vehicle clattered out the road.

"You can take better care of her than her mother," he said. "You saw the state of that man's dogs. He should be shot, or better, whipped and starved to death. But the breeding is good. With you and your kids, the puppy will thrive. She'll live like a queen."

"Why, Gabriel, that's a great name for her, Victoria, for the queen of England. We'll call her Vicky."

At their first meeting, Penny sniffed her eagerly then sighed with ineffable sadness because it wasn't Schultz, and returned to the courtyard to watch for the return of her friend. She accepted the tiny puppy's presence and tolerated her attempts at play, but very firmly made it clear that her affections were engaged elsewhere.

From her first day, Vicky seemed to realize the enormous burden placed on her. She followed in footsteps of greatness, those of Schultz, but with the wisdom of the very young, didn't even try filling them. She, quite simply, made her own place in our hearts with her gentle, loving nature.

The little creature had an enormous appetite, making up for a lifetime, short though it might be, of deprivation. It wasn't long before warm milk, fresh eggs and ground meat with rice filled in between her ribs and her coat shone like a cedar chest rubbed to a high gloss.

It was a proud moment for us both when she, with royal dignity, placed the tailfeathers of the rooster at my feet.

Vicky was only a few months old when Gabriel's largesse struck again. My first inkling that someone had arrived at the farm came when I heard our little dog wailing in terror. I went out to see who was there. Vicky was still wailing from her refuge under the car. She was certain the King Kong of dogs had arrived and she was doomed.

In the courtyard, I found Gabriel and Jerry, an impressive, white Great Pyrenees sheepdog weighing ninety pounds at least, although only a year old and still growing. He moved calmly and with great dignity through the courtyard, inspecting these new surroundings with interest and ignoring the ineffectual howls emanating from under the car.

Jerry's first owners had acquired him as an adorable puppy, a puff ball of white fur, and watched, appalled, as he grew larger than a full-grown sheep to nearly the size of a small pony or a locomoting snowdrift. They traded in their sports car for a station wagon to accommodate him, but their apartment was simply not tradeable and, with regret, they were searching for a new and more appropriate home for their pet. Gabriel assured them he had the perfect spot for Jerry and proudly presented the dog to us. The children were ecstatic and, even I, after looking into his sad brown eyes, fell in love with the huge dog.

A magnificent animal, the only color on his body was the black 'mascara' outlining his intelligent, wide-set eyes. Looking much like a polar bear with floppy ears, he moved regally, his fluffy plumed tail coiled proudly above his back.

Jerry rapidly made himself at home, although it was many months before any of us was allowed to caress or even touch his head, his last bastion of intimacy. Hugging, pats on his back, all other caresses were accepted with a gentle swing of the huge tail. Penny tolerated him, but let him know that her heart, having been given to Schultz, was not available. Jerry, however, adored Vicky and adopted her as his very own. He courted her with gentleness until she curled up between his enormous paws. Then he bathed her entire body with one sweep of his tongue.

Our nearest neighbors up the hill, Monsieur and Madame Saint-Martin, met him early on when he ventured through the fields and woods between our properties and presented himself at their door. His friendly, laughing face and wagging tail belied his size and soon they were stocking assorted biscuits and treats for their new friend. Vicky was not nearly as venturesome as Jerry, so one day he simply picked her up by the scruff of her neck, took her with him up the hill and laid her proudly, and wetly, at their feet, much like a new father.

Our mailman delivered the mail in a small Citröen, closely pulling up to the mailbox—which was nailed to a large oak and so terrorized my horse, Bambi—and passing the mail out the car window into the box. He fancied himself a ladies' man and was a petite dandy, thus earning the nickname, *"Bijou"* (jewel). He was terrified of dogs.

Jerry found the whole process fascinating and set off down the lane each day at mailtime to await *Bijou*. Sitting himself squarely in front of the mailbox, he watched for the little car. When it arrived he would stand up and wag his tail, smiling happily, as *Bijou* attempted to approach the box without leaving the safety of his car. After much horn honking, motor racing and a bark or two, Jerry would allow him to position the car next to the mailbox while he raced up the hill to meet him again at the Saint-Martin's mailbox and start the game all over again.

Jerry had never been on a farm before, but his expression as he watched the cows showed that the inbred instincts of generations of herd dogs lurked deep in his subconscious. Unfortunately, with no experience or training he hadn't a clue as to how to proceed. He tried barking, but was sharply reprimanded and his sensitive nature immediately registered that as a no-no. He observed thoughtfully as twice daily the milk cows were brought in to the barn and then taken back out to the field. I learned to close him in the kitchen before bringing in the cows so as not to frighten the placid beasts, as well as to show him that the cows were not his concern.

During the year, the cows were moved from field to field as the pastures were grazed, to provide feed for the animals and to allow the fields to re-grow. At the moment, my little herd was pastured in an outlying field through at least two separate fences and gates. Only one afternoon, they weren't. All ten of the girls, along with the group of eight yearlings and another twenty or so strange cows, were bellowing and stomping around the gate to the courtyard while a very proud Jerry raced from side to side, keeping them firmly in place at the gate. The magnificent white plume waved regally over his back and he truly believed that he was finally doing the work for which he had been bred.

I wished for lightning to strike, tried tapping my heels together while muttering, "I want to go home, I want to go home." No luck. Cars were already pulling into my courtyard dispersing angry neighboring farmers, followed by the ever-cheerful Gabriel.

"*Quel rascal du chien!*" (What a rascal of a dog!) He shook his head, chuckling.

I set to work, first grabbing Jerry by the collar and depositing him in the kitchen behind closed doors. He looked at me in shock and disbelief, tail now dragging pitifully on the floor. Next I sorted out my ladies, leading them into their barn where they could calm down over a dinner of oats and alfalfa hay. The frolicking yearlings were escorted into a neighboring stall filled with fresh hay. My neighbors were attempting to sort out their herds, using a pungent combination of French and *patois*, whole bunches of words I'd never learned, but from their facial expressions and gestures they were quite readily understood. I grimaced, thinking, *My boys would have loved this*. I was glad they were in school.

Gabriel and I followed the group heading to the south in order to repair the fences through which Jerry had simply run the cows. He apparently felt that every cow in the neighborhood must, of course, belong to us and was bringing them home—through electric fences and all! He didn't do gates. My abject apologies were brushed off. Americans, particularly a woman, couldn't be expected to know any better. However, I had better never let this happen again! Only Gabriel saw any humor in the situation.

After this momentous rebuke, Jerry totally ignored the cows, turning his head and refusing even to look at them when they passed through the courtyard. For him, they had ceased to exist. However, once again, all the chickens were without tail feathers.

Jerry was not a dog to lie quietly and nap his life away. He needed work and exercise. Our fifty acres was okay, as far as it went, but he decided the entire hillside, from the Saint-Martins at the top down to the village at the bottom, required his attention and investigation. This covered about a mile of real estate, including a couple of small sheep farms.

Gabriel also covered a lot of ground. He and his wife rented a house in the valley, but he helped his elderly uncle farm the family property up and over the hill. His vineyard occupied another field some distance from that and he helped a brother who raised sheep on our hillside. For Gabriel, this was an ideal situation. He could never be pinned down to one location at any given time.

"*Mais non*, I was with *l'oncle* after lunch. We had to move *les vaches* to the back field." or "*Bien sûr, mon frère* needed my help." Gabriel had an excuse to be anywhere or nowhere while he visited with cronies or paused for *un coup de rouge*.

On a couple of occasions he picked up Jerry on the road between *Vezat* and the village and returned him home.

"Guess where I found this *rascal du chien?*"

Both Jerry and Gabriel stood there grinning at some huge shared joke.

Then the sheep killer struck and the neighbors down the hill decided it must be that dog of *l'Americaine*. He was big, wasn't he? He was white, wasn't he? *Tous le monde* knows she has such a dog. Such a giant! *Ah, oui! Mais certainement!* And he runs loose on the hillside. He's the killer.

The next day, Gabriel brought me the bad news. The entire village wanted my dog shot.

"But, Gabriel, no." I sobbed. "He couldn't. He wouldn't. He does mischievous things because he wants to help and doesn't know any better. But he's no killer. No."

I tried to think. "When did the attack take place?" I asked.

"The other night. Monday. While the farmer slept. He was up before dawn and saw the dog slink away from the dead animal. A big white dog."

Relief settled on me like a coronation cloak. "It's not him, don't you see? He sleeps inside, with us. He didn't go out until daylight, when I got up to milk, and he stayed with me the whole time until I took the kids to school. Gabriel," I babbled in my joy, "Gabriel, it wasn't him."

Gabriel carried this information to the village. They didn't believe it for a minute. I was a foreigner. But they gave me the benefit of the doubt. Until the next attack.

I decided to take strong preventive action to remove Jerry from suspicion. I would have to stop his roaming. Jerry was hard to fence in, especially since the courtyard opened to the lane and then to the road to the village. Everyone drove in and out. But this was serious. This was war. Jerry had to be contained for his own good. We had learned, quite by accident, that Jerry had a terror of the electric fences surrounding the cows. So we surrounded every opening from the courtyard with triple electric wires and built a gate at the lane for bringing in cars, tractors, mopeds, etc, etc.

We weren't being cruel; touching the wire would in no way have resulted in a fried dog. Not even in curling his hair. If any part of his body had touched the wire, covered as it was by that thick coat of fur, he would not have felt more than a tickle. At some point in his roamings, however, Jerry must have touched the wire with his tender *truffe*, that moist black nose, and given himself a jolt. And when Jerry learned something, it stayed learned.

That's where matters stood when the second sheep was killed. This time the evil deed was committed just over the hill, within two miles of us. A delegation from the village arrived at the gate. Jerry sat inside.

"Your dog, Madame, *votre chien*. He has killed another sheep," they announced, with certainty.

"But he is fenced. You see for yourself. He has not left the property," I held his collar and did not offer to open the gate.

"This fence," a wide expansive, very French gesture, "cannot contain a dog like this." A few chuckles, dismissing the *parvenu*. *Les femmes!* Americans!

I looked up to see Gabriel's rattletrap car jolting, rattling, bouncing down the lane. Jerry barked joyously. I felt like the marines had landed, the cavalry had ridden up. I swear I heard trumpets. My knight in shining armor had some problem opening his car door, but finally the heel of his hand contacted the magic spot with sufficient force, the door flew open and he strode out.

"*Eh bien, les gars.*" He slapped a few backs and gripped several hands, then let himself in the gate, closing it firmly behind, allying himself with me and the animal at my side, the one that was bouncing around him, licking his hands and generally acting like an overgrown pup.

He pushed Jerry down and turned to face the delegation.

"*Alors,* did you see the fence? *C'est merveilleux, n'est-ce pas?*"

My champion may not have been a pillar of the community, but he was French and a friend of the village men from childhood. Many of them had fought with him in the *maquis*, the underground fighters who continued operations long after France surrendered to the Nazis and was occupied during World War II. The men shuffled their feet, they muttered, they milled around, nodding and admiring my fine fence. Then they left.

But as they were getting into their cars, the spokesman turned.

"Next time, Madame, next time the dog dies. *Salut, Gabriel.*"

Gabriel nudged me into the kitchen. A glass of wine was called for.

"Vous inquietez pas. Le chien sera sage." He refilled his glass and downed it, then shook his head. *"Quel rascal!"* And he was off, chuckling.

"Don't worry. The dog will be good." Hah! Might as well say Jerry would suddenly start singing grand opera. I had an uneasy feeling that if the villagers hauled off our big, white hound and shot him, World War III wouldn't be far behind. The Archduke and Jerry might have a lot in common!

Sleeping that night was impossible—one long nightmare. I kept seeing Jerry with a blindfold and groups of men wearing berets aiming rifles at him. I got up and walked out to the field, hoping the cows and the rabbits and the resident owls would calm me. But I couldn't sit still and my restlessness scared off the rabbits and the owl and the cows just didn't understand the situation. Besides, it was too damned cold.

By morning, my disposition rivaled that of the Wicked Witch of the West. Two of my placid, gentle cows kicked me during milking and I knocked over a bucket of milk. The kids were delighted to be delivered to school, a haven of peace. They didn't understand the situation either.

Jerry, looking as though he had a clear conscience, was regally surveying his kingdom from the top of a pile of hay. He was well out of range of the flying turds and soiled bedding straw emerging from the calf barn where I was trying to wear myself out and forestall another white night, when Gabriel's car clunked into the lane.

Jerry erupted into welcoming joy and I emerged, wiping perspiration from my face.

Gabriel bounded out of the car, hugged Jerry and hollered in my direction, "*C'est fini*. They found the killer. It's over. Got any coffee?" He headed for the kitchen.

I stood there, pitchfork in hand, mouth open. That's it? It's over? Got any coffee? Leaning the pitchfork against the barn wall, I followed him in to reheat the coffee. The French don't care how strong the coffee is. To them, three-day-old coffee is just approaching a good strength.

He grabbed my bottle of *eau de vie* and filled half the glass before the coffee even touched it. The local brandy made from plums was Gabriel's sole reason for wanting the coffee. Enough of this stuff and he was back in his teens in the *maquis* blowing up bridges and holding off battalions of Nazis. It was rumored in the village that some of the locals had collaborated with the Nazis, but Gabriel would only answer my questions with "What's past is past."

"Gabriel," I couldn't stand it any longer as I topped off the brandy with coffee. "Gabriel, what happened?"

He blew on the potent mixture and drank down a hearty slug. "The dog attacked the same flock last night," he said, wiping his mouth with the back of his hand. "But this time the farmer was waiting, rifle in hand. He didn't miss. It was a big, white dog, but not this one." He ruffled the heavy fur on Jerry's neck. "A shame, you know, once they get the taste... Gotta go. *L'oncle* needs me." He drained the glass and headed back out.

"Gabriel," I called. "Gabriel, thanks once again."

He turned and smiled, then was gone.

There were two sure things. One, the men from the village would never admit they were wrong, certainly not to me. And second, without Gabriel's help, Jerry would be dead.

Friendship is a wondrous thing. It's a plant that sets its roots deep within two hearts, branches leafing and flowering between them. If the roots are not properly nourished in one of the hearts, the plant suffers and dies. I had friends like that in the States. Friends who no longer knew me after my husband left. Friends with no time to answer letters, to share lives.

Gabriel and I had no shared background. I couldn't even imagine his early life, nor he mine. He had been very young when the Germans came through Saint-Cyprien, gathering men and boys. His older brother was caught and sent to a labor camp. Gabriel, being Gabriel, was playing hooky from school that day and he escaped the round-up. That was when he joined the *maquis* and, a mere boy, became an underground freedom fighter.

Gabriel and I shared only a lively sense of the ridiculous; we each laughed easily, perhaps to cover deeper wounds. But if I needed help, a listening ear or a hearty chuckle, I knew where to find it. My heart felt a ray of warmth.

I hugged Jerry and realized he was allowing me to scratch the top of his smooth rounded head, to wiggle my fingers around the soft ears. Not only allowing me, he was leaning into my hand. Another friend. *Quel rascal!*

❧ CHAPTER 26 ❧

Another Letter Home

Dear Pat,

Thank you, again, for the box of goodies. We all loved the sweatshirts and, of course, the Mexican foodstuffs. But, most of all, at least from me, thank you thank you thank you for the paperback books. Escaping into Mary Stewart, Victoria Holt or Georgette Heyer is like slipping into another life, more elegant and more exciting, where all problems are nicely tied up by the last page. I feel as if I'll never personally reach that last chapter.

We are at this moment overrun with cats. Too bad they're not a cash crop, we would eat hearty for the next year. I have to admit they earn their keep. The mouse population keeps pretty much out of sight, which is where I prefer them. I know there are a few rats, because the cats regularly leave me the gift of a bloody corpse under the corn grinder in the attic. I'm impressed. Those critters are as big as the cats.

Anyway, about the population explosion. Minette and her eldest daughter, Cleo, both kittened (is that a word?) within a week of each other. Minette was a tender mom with her first litter, while her second was, fortunately, an only child, because she refused to have anything to do with the poor little fellow. This time there are three and I'm simply forcing her to nurse the babies several times a day. She'd be just as happy to let Cleo take over and Cleo is sweet enough to try, but I think it's unreasonable. After all, she has three of her own.

As if that weren't enough, our friends, Jane and René, asked us if we could adopt three more orphaned babies, "as long as you have two nursing mums." Nine blind, mewling kittens in one box is enough to scare off any sensible mother cat, but Cleo, bless her gentle feline heart, spends hours bathing and fussing over each and every one. The very least Minette can do is share a few of the feeding chores, although she gives me heartrending looks whenever I dump her into the pile. I've made her supper conditional on it.

Over and above these, of course, are a couple of lazy adult males, the cause of the whole problem (except for the orphans and, who knows, *Saint Pompon* isn't THAT far away), and our simple-minded Siamese. Speaking of dumb old Pasha, he nearly got himself buried alive the other day. Just for taking a nap in a tractor tread.

The kids were at school, I was picking up the daily bread and the local entrepreneur was baling the hay in the back field when Gabriel drove in. Gabriel has never understood my adoration of Pasha, that silly beast. He thinks Siamese are scrawny, useless and downright ugly. And heaven knows, Pasha certainly does nothing to prove him wrong.

He's the only cat I've ever known who can fall down and land on his back. Then simply lie there. I guess you just have to love him!

The ground at the entrance into the back field was still a bit mushy from rains last week and the heavy baling machine left deep tire ruts in the earth. Smooth, rounded, soft and sun-warmed. A perfect spot for a catnap.

Pasha is shaped very Siamese-like and bone skinny. Gabriel glimpsed him lying in the depression and immediately assumed he'd been squashed by the entrepreneur's baling machine. M'sieur Lariviere has been charged with many things, but I don't think running over pet cats is one of them. And much as Gabriel may have felt personal satisfaction over the loss of the one critter he considered useless, his heart was soft enough to know that I would be devastated. Or, more likely, he couldn't bear the thought of coping with my tears.

He'd grabbed a shovel and started digging a grave when I drove in. Running down to intercept me before I found the body, he solemnly led me to view the remains, which were stretching luxuriously and eyeing us with a pair of crossed blue eyes.

Well, enough about cats.

Pat, the next time you turn the dreaded forty, you must do it in France. Here, you are treated like you've been selected for membership in an elite sorority. Far from being looked at as over the hill and well past the age of desirability, I'm now getting interested glances and suspect invitations even from the pharmacist.

Pharmacists here provide first aid services and will recommend medicines for minor ailments, like coughs and headaches. I don't think they can actually prescribe, but potions like cough syrup or aspirin with codeine are available over the counter. I was back somewhere between toothpaste and Tampax when *M'sieur le Pharmacien* appeared, whispering that he would be happy to deliver my purchases so I wouldn't be burdened. I assured him that a nasal spray and Band-Aids wouldn't be too much for my frail strength, so he breathily suggested dinner some evening. I smiled broadly and assured him the children would be delighted, since they already knew his kids, and I would look forward to meeting his wife. At which point, he was suddenly called back to the counter. Such a friendly community! Do you think I'll hear from him again?

Tim is collecting signatures on the cast on his right wrist. That boy has seen more hospital emergency rooms in his meager years than most people do in a lifetime. At least five visits in three different countries. This time, he broke his wrist while walking on a paved road. Tripped over his own feet. One of his friends ran up to the farm to get me and, funny thing, I'd been plowing a field when suddenly my right wrist hurt so badly I had to stop. What amazing prescience mothers have!

Jerry, our big dog, has been behaving himself. Well, as much as is possible for him. He's still terrified of the electric fence, so three flimsy wires around the courtyard are containing him. I have no confidence that situation will last.

Every evening the local owls play games with him. That is, it's either several owls located on both ends of the courtyard or one owl flying back and forth. In any case, the hoots start at one end, he runs toward it barking, then the hoots move to the other and he runs toward that end and then back again. After about half an hour of hooting and running and barking, the owls go back to hunting, with a good chuckle at his expense, I'm sure, and he retires in great dignity to the pile of straw in front of the barn.

The children and I took a trip to Les Eyzies one day last week to see the cave drawings. When prehistoric skeletons were unearthed there in 1868, the market town of Les Eyzies-de-Tayac became an archaeologist's dream. This area of the Dordogne Valley was found to be a treasure trove of ancient sites, mostly found in the caves, where our early ancestors drew primitive animal shapes and symbols on the walls and coarsely carved images on rocks.

If you recall, Pat, during my life in the United States, I loved visiting old cemeteries, reading the inscriptions and musing on long-gone people and events. I was fascinated when we visited an old burial ground in Tombstone, Arizona, where the dead from the Battle at the OK Corral were buried, along with other early settlers and adventurers. The grave markers contained dates like 1874 and 1881.

In New Jersey, we stopped one fall afternoon at a cemetery beside an old stone church. The plots were surrounded by a wrought iron fence with pointy spikes, but there was a gate and a narrow stone-lined path through the graves. I pushed trailing weeds away from the weathered tombstones and read epitaphs and dates in the 1700s and was terribly impressed.

Now, I find myself in a country with artifacts dating back to before recorded history. There are caves with paintings done in vivid red and yellow ochres that date from 17,000 B.C. That's *before* Christ! I really had trouble wrapping my mind around that.

The sheer limestone cliffs lining the banks of the Dordogne are pitted with natural shelters and caves that have been used by man for more than 400,000 years. Man settled in these areas because they provided a shelter for living, water, rivers filled with fish, a game-filled hinterland but, more important still, rich flint seams providing the vital raw materials for the rudimentary arms or tools required for survival. Cro-Magnon Man was discovered here, as well as relics from the Neanderthal and Magdalanian eras. From Montignac to Le Bugue, there are twenty-five decorated caves and one hundred and fifty prehistoric sites spread over a distance of less than eighteen miles. *La Font de Gaume*, one mile south of Les Eyzies, contains superb engravings of bison, mammoths, horses and stags. *Les Combarelles* is incomparable for the richness and variety of its mural art containing almost eight hundred engravings along a gallery 325 yards long.

Prehistory did not come to a halt with the end of the Paleolithic Age. Périgord also has major remains dating from the late Stone Age and the Bronze or Iron Ages.

At the front of the cave at Les Eyzies stands a giant stone carving of Cro-Magnon Man, whose remains were found in this region. There seem to be a large number of prehistoric relics around here. I don't know if that indicates the caves were the perfect spot for preserving them, or if this was really the Birthplace of Man, as many of the locals insist.

The caves, or *les grottes* as they're called here, are cool and damp and the guides use special lights so as not to affect the paintings. The paintings themselves, mostly of horses, bison and other animals, are in vivid reds, greens and purples. It's hard to believe they made these colors from berries and other vegetation. After spending the greater part of my life in a country with a sparse few centuries of recorded history, I'm still in awe of this place, where tombstones have incredible dates of five and six hundred years ago and there exist still some Gaullic ruins, dry stone huts, built before the Roman conquest and about the same time Jesus walked around Galilee. There is even a huge table-shaped stone dolmen, a relic of their ancient worship.

I've dropped in these cultural tidbits so you won't think all my dealings with cow poop have turned my brain to mush. Actually, kids can have the same effect.

Thanks again, my dear, not only for the box of goodies, but for the love and friendship in your letters. We're so far away, but they bring all of you right here to our kitchen. A cup of tea, your letter and, magically, we're together.

Love always,

Jan

❧ CHAPTER 27 ❧

Each Passing Season

We often had a false spring in February, two or three perfect weeks, the sun bringing warmth and golden light to a barren landscape. The birds trilled their joy and fruit trees, lulled by the siren, budded and flowered. In the woods, smack in the midst of oak and juniper, I was startled by a blooming plum, its masses of white like an improbable snowfall. I pictured a thieving jay snatching the juicy fruit from one of the trees lining the lane, sucking the sweet pulp and chucking the pit into the woods where it landed then sprouted in the rich soil, nourished by rain and cosseted by a covering of leaves.

March and April invariably brought freezing rains, sleet, even snow. The birds went wherever cold birds go, the land froze and crystallized and we mourned the last of the year's crop of fruit, dead in blackened blossoms on the trees.

Life at *Vezat* had settled into a routine for us, governed by the seasons. Summer's end was marked by the *vendange*.

If we'd been lucky to have any summer rains, there would be a final haying, the last picnics on the banks of the Dordogne River with swims in the cool, smoothly flowing current and perhaps even a picnic at the smaller Céou River with its clear, icy waters and sudden, deep pools. Fall held the harvest of the tobacco, placed into great plastic-covered drying sheds or hung on lines in open barns. I praised heaven regularly that I didn't raise tobacco, lucrative though it might be. That crop required far too much expertise for a novice like me.

As the boys reached their teens, they worked during vacations for the big tobacco growers from dawn to dusk until school started. Another job that helped provide them with the means to fuel their mopeds and finance other teenage requirements was working for the local produce seller in Saint-Cyprien. This required weekly visits to the regional market at Sarlat, which forced them to drag themselves out of warm beds in the wee hours—not an easy job during those fragile teen years when their biological clocks normally don't tick at all before noon.

We alternated plantings of rye and corn annually in our plowed fields in an effort to replace some of the nutrients in the soil, occasionally even varying with a planting of alfalfa. The grains were needed for the animals. On rye growing years, late fall saw the arrival of the big harvesting machine which beat the grains out and dropped the straw back onto the field for later raking and baling, to be used for bedding in the barns. Corn took longer and frost was already sprinkling the fields when the corn-picker arrived.

René designed and supervised the building of the big corn crib we erected beside the lane, a large wire rack which held the husked cobs for drying. Later, they were run through the *engreneur* to remove the grains from the cobs and store in bags or barrels in the attic.

Gabriel rattled into the lane during the building process and seized the opportunity to heckle.

"*Eh bien,* you should've put it over there, the other side of the field."

"*Gros con,*" René rose instantly to the bait, "what d'you know?"

I brought out a bottle of wine to distract them and nipped that argument at the start.

The fields were plowed after the harvest, turning under the corn husks and stalks and any remaining straw, and allowed to lie fallow throughout the winter. One year the fall rains were so heavy, the machine harvesters were unable to enter the corn field and picking needed to be done by hand. I thought we'd never finish the job and, believe me, once for that job was enough! I regularly consulted René's almanac before planting corn again. I was willing to accept any help I could get.

René said, "*Eh Oui*! You're learning."

By December we were gathering walnuts from under the trees lining the lane. These were spread to dry in large wire racks built into wood frames on short legs in the attic. When dry, the husks were removed and the nuts were bagged to be sold at market. Gabriel usually took care of this for me or sent a merchant up to buy them directly. I would, no doubt, have done better if I'd sold them at market myself, but my hawking skills were never great and I was no match for the natives.

December and January saw the birth of new calves and was a time for seeking new babies to raise. Some years I bought half a dozen in a group from a merchant, but mostly I visited neighboring farms and bought promising young heifers, one here, one there. Each year I gained confidence in my selection abilities, but I was always a sucker for a sweet baby face.

The early months of the new year were spent in twice daily milk feedings of the baby calves, often four-hourly feedings of orphaned baby lambs, checking for new litters of bunnies, calf barn cleaning, fence repairs, pruning and tying up the grapevines, fertilizing hay fields, the myriad chores for which there is never any time during the growing and harvesting months. The milking herd was moved from one outlying field to another as feed was slurped from every possible surface.

By early spring, the grain fields were re-plowed, raked, fertilized and planted. In May the haying cycles started again. There always seemed to be something that needed doing, but it was always something different. It occurred to me that one would need to be a farmer for a long time to get bored with the limitless variety of chores and challenges, not to mention long-term problems and sudden catastrophes.

It was a constant learning experience. My strategy was first to ask Gabriel, then another neighbor and, finally, one of the bigger farmers from the valley. After carefully considering these three frequently very different options, I'd decide what would work best for me and do it. In each case, a success would be met by, "See, what'd I tell you? Follow my advice and you won't go wrong," from all three. Failures were greeted with, "Why didn't you do what I told you to do? *Eh bien,* next time you'll know better," from each of the trio, no matter their original advice.

Sometime during the summer was also the time for Rob's annual visit with the children. Though we were permanently separated, Rob kept up the same "less is more" parenting regime he had earlier initiated after he'd dropped us in France. The first year of our "official" separation, Rob came over and spent a couple of weeks at the farm, bunking with Danny and finishing up his building projects. Then, after the printing company died a slow agonizing death, he resumed his gypsy ways and accepted a position in Iran. Over the next few years, he alternated visits with the boys and the girls, one year sending tickets for the boys to visit him, the following year it was the girls' turn to visit wherever he happened to be.

The kids became international travelers. Singly or in pairs, they traveled to Washington D.C., Spain, Iran, Bahrain and Kuwait to spend time with their father. During one of their jaunts, the plane the boys were on stopped briefly for refueling in Beirut and they were told they could walk around outside to stretch their legs. When the boys descended the stairs, they looked out to find the plane ringed by armed militia, rifles trained directly on the plane. They turned back, deciding their legs didn't need stretching after all.

The evenings I was alone, I spent a lot of time in the field sitting under the oak watching the stars, feeling a kinship with their steady motion, their dance across the heavens. As I reviewed my past and present and wondered about the future, I realized everything we touch, each life we cross, remains an element in our sphere as we traverse our allotted time.

Nodding at those sparkling celestial beacons, I got up and went inside to join the cats in bed.

∽ CHAPTER 28 ∾

Horse Shit

I met one of Gabriel's friends who was a relative newcomer; he'd only been in the Dordogne region since the 1940s. His family lived in Normandy before the war, but he and his sister were the only surviving members and the property in Normandy was long gone. They were still, and would forever be, in the eyes of the villagers, *les Normandais*.

The brother and sister worked their farm together. Gabriel called him Patou, I called him M'sieur. He was small and wiry, too shy to look me in the eye, but with a quick grin and a burbly chuckle. Only a few tufts of hair remained around the edges of his head and he regularly removed his beret to rub his scalp. He felt it aided thought. Madame was a full head taller and many kilos heavier, but equally good-humored. She'd been a young girl studying at the Cordon Bleu school in Paris when France fell to Germany. When cold and starvation came too close, she made her way to the

Dordogne and her brother, her only surviving relative. Together, they bought their small farm and produced vegetables for the local markets and restaurants. Asparagus was their specialty.

The prime fertilizer for asparagus is horse manure. In this region of sheep and dairy farms, there weren't many horses. Perhaps the occasional work horse kept for tilling a *vigne*, but they shared quarters with the cows. According to the *paysans*, the manure was best if it was pure.

I was more than happy to donate the pure product of our horses. I refused any payment for something I was delighted to have hauled off the property, but was not averse to accepting the hospitality of a meal. After all, Madame was a graduate of Cordon Bleu.

Gabriel and M'sieur were already hard at work when I returned from delivering the kids to school. They'd hooked up the *remorque* to the tractor and backed it into the courtyard and were forking large chunks of the valuable stuff produced effortlessly by our great, lazy horses. As the load rose, Gabriel paused and eyed it warily.

"*Cette merde pese.*" This shit is heavy. "Don't want to load too much or you'll never make it up the hill. You sure you can make the turn?" He glanced at the spot where our lane joined the main road. The lane was carved out of the hillside, with the fields falling away below. The opposite side of the narrow road was sheer cliff. The angle formed at the junction of the roads was about 45 degrees. I'd have to turn the tractor back and nearly meet the *remorque* still going the other way. And all while going uphill.

I laughed. "Sure, Gabriel. Heck, I do it all the time."

"*Bien sûr.* But not with a remorque loaded with horse shit. You'll have to make it first try. You won't get a second chance. Miss the turn and you'll be pulled backwards down the hill." He didn't look happy.

"*Patou, ca suffit,*" Gabriel called out to his friend. "If you need more, we'll come back." He shoved his pitchfork firmly in the black yuck and put his hand on my shoulder. "*Ça va, Janine?* You want me to drive the tractor?"

I smiled, cocky and sure of myself, as only the truly uninformed can be. "*Oui, Gabriel. Ça va.* I'll be fine. Just watch."

"Okay. Patou and I'll go ahead and wait on the road. I'll guide you around." And they rattled off as I shoved the dogs in the kitchen and climbed onto the tractor seat.

The sun shone brightly, birds argued vociferously over heaven-knew-what. Since the birds were French, I had no doubt they were discussing politics. The cows grazed in the field below the barn, some already settling down for a midday nap in the shade at the edge of the woods. The river curved through the valley below. As Gabriel's nervousness transmitted itself to the pit of my stomach, I decided the cows had the right idea.

I started up the ever-increasing incline on the lane and felt the tug of the loaded *remorque. Oh, oui, cette merde pese.* Gabriel trotted down the lane toward me, waving wildly to indicate that I was to swing as wide as possible to make the turn. I swung out and started the turn, pressing steadily on the gas to maintain enough speed.

The tractor was straining, but pulling steadily. The Little Engine That Could chugged up the hill valiantly. I

swung the wheel hard left and prayed. I was beginning to feel
the danger. About time. If it went wrong, this could, I realized, be my chance to bag this world of cares and woes. But
under a load of horse shit?

Gabriel scrambled up the embankment. From the corner of my eye, I saw him motioning, but I was fully occupied
with my own problems. On the cliff-side, the tractor wheel
had come plumb against a jutting rock. I knew if the tractor
stopped, if I needed to maneuver clutch, brake, gas, it would
roll backwards and over. Don't even think about trying to
backup, shift gears and go forward again. Once I took my foot
off the gas, the weight of the manure would send me and the
remorque over the bank and down the hill.

I stomped harder on the gas and the front of the tractor reared like a prancing horse. Oh my God! Maintaining
pressure on the gas pedal, I leaned forward, partially standing.
At least I'd go down fighting. I could smell rubber burning and
hear gravel pinging off the underside of the equipment. The
engine shrieked like a handful of fingernails on a blackboard.

The tractor settled back to the ground, this time in
front of the obstructive rock and slowly, steadily pulled
around the bend and up the hill. I think I can. I think I can. I
know I can. Hallelujah, brother!

When the road leveled off at the crown of the hill, I
pulled off at the first wide spot and cut the engine. My legs
felt like yarn and began to tremble. Gabriel jumped up beside
me and held my face between his two hands. His face was a
peculiar ash-grey.

"Mon Dieu, mon Dieu!" he kept repeating. Then he
brightened and chuckled. *"Allons-y.* What we need is a *bon
coup de rouge."*

Patou pulled ahead and Gabriel climbed on. I forced some starch back into my legs and started my valiant machine. The rest of the trip was a breeze and we were soon pulling into the neatest little farm I'd yet seen. The tiny house sat next to the road, painted white. Fields marched along the side in perfect squares, rows of plants in geometric lines, straight in all directions. Regimented drill teams.

The sunny promise of the day had turned into grey drizzle. Weather in the Dordogne changed with the frequency and abruptness of mood changes in a hormonal teenager. At Patou's direction, I pulled beside a neatly rowed field. He kept his head down but managed arm signals until I jumped down and ran for the shelter of the house.

Madame pulled me in, shoved me in front of a cheerful fire and, before I realized it, I had a large glass of wine clutched in my hand. And, oh, the delicious smells! There was garlic, of course, and herbs and spices. I've always been what you might call cooking-challenged and haven't a clue as to which ingredient is what. But like an art connoisseur, I know what I like. This I liked.

The room was small, but immaculate. The wide plank floor practically glowed. A long table filled the center of the room, with blue-flowered crockery settings for four. A black kettle hung on a chain from a hook deep within the fireplace simmering something ambrosia-like. Heat emanated from an old wood stove with several more pots bubbling. A washed pine table under the window contained a few mixing bowls and a terra cotta pot of blue hyacinth just starting to bloom.

It took me a few minutes to realize what was missing. A sink. This kitchen contained no running water. And we were about to eat what promised to be the gourmet meal of my life.

A gust of cold, wet air brought Gabriel and Patou inside, grabbing for towels hanging on hooks beside the door. Must've been a pump outside because their hands and faces were dripping from more than rain. As I took a chair at the long table with my back to the fire, a calico kitten climbed my leg, circled twice on my lap and settled herself comfortably. I stroked the soft fur and felt the contented rumble. Wonderful medicine. My heartbeat was almost back to normal.

Madame served big steaming bowls of *soupe aux poireaux,* a creamy blend of potato, onion and cream. In that region, custom dictates that after the soup, one does a *chabrol.* This involves placing the spoon curved side up in the bowl and covering it with wine, then drinking the wine directly from the soup bowl. I went along, but with just enough wine to pull off the remaining succulent bits from the bowl.

"Gabriel, this tastes like your wine," I said, raising my head from the bowl with, I was sure, a soup-wine moustache.

He looked at me as one would regard a pup who, for the first time, scratches to be let out rather than peeing behind the sofa. Apparently, I was showing signs that I might turn out all right after all. This was certainly my day.

The rest of the meal passed in a haze of *pâté de campagne, asperges vinaigrettes, entrecôte grillée à la Périgourdine, civet de lapin, crêpes flambés,* followed, of course, by platters of fruit and cheese of all sorts. Gabriel on one side and Patou on the other made sure my wine glass never dropped below half and the wine and alcohol content of the sauces was enough to render a savant incoherent.

I convinced Gabriel that I really did not want my coffee loaded with *eau de vie* and clambered up onto my tractor ready to negotiate the road home. I don't remember much about the ride home except for fleeting mental images of a movie I once saw of three trucks carrying explosives to a forest fire, in which two of the trucks blew sky high en route. The third arrived successfully, after nail-biting, seat-edge-sitting tension, unloaded the explosives and headed home, the driver carefree and singing, only to miss a turn and crash down the mountainside.

I got home just in time for evening milking.

Soul Food

For four years I'd wrestled with the elemental necessities of survival: food, shelter, clothing, education. And I appeared to be winning. Or at least it was a tie-game. *Vezat* now had electricity, a sink with water which ran from a faucet (both hot and cold!) with a drain which connected to underground pipes and a septic tank, an **indoor** toilet, as well as a real shower almost fully enclosed. To be honest, the walls didn't quite meet the roof at the upper levels, making showering in winter a spartan experience and definitely cutting down on any thought of leisurely reading on the potty. A telephone was still a distant dream, but I'd forgotten why I wanted one.

As for education, we also had a television set which received two channels. The signal for the third channel emanated from the other side of the hill in back of our house. Sound made it. Picture didn't. And we understood every word! Except maybe the politicians' rhetoric.

Now my soul wanted feeding. I needed a piano. I yearned for its companionship, the joy of sharing my deepest emotions and innermost concerns with an instrument which echoed its voice back to mine and provided release from stress and fears. I had studied off and on since the age of five and found playing provided an emotional outlet unlike any other. The highs and lows of love found expression in the lyrical romanticism of Schumann and Chopin and when life became really difficult, nothing straightened out my thinking like the purity of Mozart or the mathematical precision of Bach.

René knew everyone in Saint-Cyprien and its environs and was related to most of them. In France, cousins are descendants of anyone who ever passed through the same village as a great grandparent. They don't bother with the twice and thrice-removed designations. Some may be even closer than they think.

René recalled a distant cousin who, at one time, had a piano and he made arrangements for us to visit. We arrived at a traditional, centuries-old farmhouse which was constructed of huge stone blocks and stone-slabbed roof. Stepping around chickens pecking on the stoop, we crouched down to pass through the low door and entered a cool, dim room dominated by a mammoth smoke-blackened fireplace with two warming benches on either side. A black iron pot hung over the smoldering embers and a small, grey cat curled herself in one of the enormous andirons. Tiny stones, time-hardened into the sand, provided the floor.

We passed through the main family living area into a newer section of the house, with plank floors and plywood partitions. This back room appeared to be a storage area with boxes, piles of burlap bags and several bags filled with grain.

Walnuts were spread out to dry across one side of the floor. Mice, rather than generations of family ghosts, occupied this part of the house. Insulation had replaced the warmth of character.

Our host, twice René's size both in height and breadth, with a pink face and pate ringed with white cherubic curls, walked to the back of the room, picked up a large pile of bags, moved several boxes and pointed proudly to a tall upright piano, so covered in dust as to be nearly unrecognizable.

"This instrument has been cherished by our family for several generations." I could tell that the piano was old, but that it had been cherished was less evident. "It was part of my grandmother's dowry. *Bon Dieu, qu'elle a aimé ce machin!*" My God, how she loved the machine! Sure. And ever since, it had collected grain sacks and provided low-rent mouse housing.

"I could maybe let it go for 2500 francs. The drought, you know, we really need to buy feed. Otherwise, we could never bear to part with it."

The wily rascal! To him it was worthless and I would be lucky if the instrument could be played and he was asking over five hundred dollars—a fortune to both of us. However, I was an American and, in his eyes, wealthy beyond belief. I didn't dare even attempt to barter. I could probably sell a cow for close to that amount, although no practical farmer would ever consider replacing a good milk cow with anything as impractical as a piano. Whoever said I was practical, much less a farmer?

The deal was made by handshake and toasted with a glass of homemade wine and I set off to decide which cow should be sacrificed for the sake of my mental health. My conscience scolded me mightily, but my mind was made up.

The day finally arrived when, with the help of more of René's cousins, we hauled it by truck to the farm and with much sweat and vivid vocabulary it was finally placed in our old house.

"Merde, j'suis foutu!" (Shit, I'm dead!)

"T'es un pauvre con!" (You're a stupid idiot!)

"Ce truc pese vachement!" (This thing weighs as much as a cow!)

"Aie!! Merde de cochon!" (*&#%^*$@!)

Linguistically, they were very creative. The boys were enchanted.

After hours of scrubbing away the years of accumulated dirt and grime, then waxing and buffing, the old mahogany case gleamed a deep burnished red. The front cabinet was ornately carved and shining brass candelabra swung out on either side of the music rack. The cabinet was a thing of beauty. However, the sounds issuing from within were sheer cacophony.

René again came to my rescue, remembering a blind piano tuner who might work on it even though retired. No doubt the man was also related to him somewhere along the line. Sure enough, through friendship for René and, I thought, boredom and curiosity, the man agreed to see what he could do. René brought him to the farm a few days later.

"But, René, how can a blind man work on this complex mechanism?" I whispered as René prepared to leave us alone together.

"Soyez tranquille! Do what he asks and for the rest, sit back and let him work." René patted my hand and roared off on his *mobylette*.

The old man was tall, with a permanent stoop as if expecting all doorways to be low. He wore the farmer's uniform of faded blues with the omnipresent beret and he was a wizard. He wore no glasses and his eyes were a clear, pale blue. They seemed vacant, like windows in an empty house. At the piano tuner's direction, I removed the front cabinet panel exposing the strings. From that moment, he needed no further assistance. He set to work with a tuning fork and a few simple tools. He might not see, but his ears heard angel choirs in perfect pitch. He worked all day and it was dusk when he sat back and rippled some full, sweet-sounding keyboard arpeggios.

"I was born blind," he said. "I went to a special school in Bordeaux and, loving the sounds of music, I elected to learn the trade of piano tuner. The final years in the school I would have learned to play, but the war came, France fell and our school was closed. Please, would you play something? Anything? I would so enjoy it. *S'il vous plaît?*"

I hadn't touched a keyboard in years, but there was no way I could refuse this gentle man who had done so much. Sitting at my new piano, I leafed through the sheet music I had brought with me from another life and time and selected Schumann's "Scenes From Childhood." The simple, lovely melodies based on a child's world—at play, dreaming, praying—with their lilting rhythms and enchanting harmonies came forth in a pure mellow sound that curled right up beside my heart. The old piano sang with a golden voice resonating in the clear evening air. As the last notes died away, the old blind man laid his rough, work worn hand on my shoulder and I reached up to cover it with mine. We each whispered one word, "*Merci*."

CHAPTER 30

Racist Cows and a Delightful Perk

Les vaches sont raciste. Cows are racist. Okay, I'll revise my statement. My cows were racist.

Honestly, that's the truth. I had a herd of gentle *Hollandaises* (Holstein) milk cows with black and white splashes. They tolerated Lily, a sweet, red-and-white speckled *Normandaise*, in their midst. All of the ladies usually were sweet-tempered and docile, and only occasionally stubborn and cranky. You know, typical PMS. Even cows get it at one time or another.

Then I decided to add a group of mixed breed yearlings, one black, a white *Charolais* and a red *Limousine*. The year had been good for alfalfa and I had an ample supply of grains, rye and corn. I planned to fatten them in pasture for a year, then sell them for beef. Sounds like I was getting the hang of this farming thing, doesn't it? Let's say I was experiencing some success.

The three calves arrived by truck and I kept them in a barn for a couple of days to get acquainted and to gain their trust by feeding them cracked corn. They were sweet, friendly youngsters, if a little shy, prancing happily in the clean straw and munching steadily on everything lying around loose.

The third day I took them out of the barn and into the open field where the milk herd grazed placidly. The three adolescents trotted happily into the lush grass but huddled closely together. The unknown is always easier faced in a group. There didn't seem to be any active hostility, so I left the girls to become acquainted and returned to my chores.

At the end of the afternoon by the time of evening milking, the groups were still maintaining their distance. I brought the ladies in to their stalls and returned the young-sters to their barn. My fences were a big improvement over Gabriel's, but I didn't have sufficient faith in them to leave the wild young things out.

At the end of a week, the young *Charolais* was grazing alongside the herd. Within the month, the *Limousine* had joined her, but let the little, black calf move close to the group and one of my docile old broads would bare her teeth and nip her away.

As I said, my cows were racist.

Farming, I had been learning, was a backbreaking, heartbreaking, unrelenting, freezing, sweaty, make-do, non-profit occupation. It is perhaps not high on everyone's list of most desirable ways of making a living. It comes with no health or dental insurance, no retirement plan, no vacations, paid or otherwise, no sick leave. The worker is entirely at the mercy of a capricious boss who, if He so desires, will fling buckets of rain at a year's worth of labor lying cut, raked and ready to bale in the field. He will then withhold rain while seedlings gasp in the dessicated soil.

On the other hand, farming has its own unique and delicious perks. What other career choice would allow me, in the middle of a summer's day, to stretch out in an open field, cupped hands under head, gazing into a blue-green sky echoing back the colors of the river and the trees? Moisture beads on my brow and pools between my breasts. A light breeze raises damp tendrils of hair. Steam rising from mown grasses scents the air. Clouds pass overhead shape-changing from rabbit to polar bear to dog to Uncle Carl. Looking deeply into, through and beyond the vastness of a celestial void, blue to green to mauve, drawing sight, being, deeper and deeper, until self disappears. Then a bird sings, clear and joyous, a cranky jay disagrees and the world reappears with a new perception of purpose, of belonging.

And I realize that a group of ants is devouring my left ankle.

cèpe

trompette-des-morts

girolle

morille

amanite tue-mouches

❧ CHAPTER 31 ❧

More Letters Home

Dear Pat,

It was wonderful receiving your letter and all the family news. Do you have any idea how welcome your letters are or how many times they get read? They make us all feel less like orphans.

I've gone and done it now! Totally destroyed my reputation, that is. Our neighbors way out on the other side of a far field, the Tabanous, are not what I'd call warm people. I guess we started off on the wrong foot when Jerry brought Tabanou's cows in with mine during the great cattle round-up. M'sieur Tabanou's sense of humor died at birth. I think his whole face would shatter if he ever smiled.

Anyway, I was working in the far field and the cows were grazing in the woods. At least, I thought they were until M'sieur Tabanou comes plodding up to the fence line and yells at me that they're in his field and I'd better get them out. *Tout de suite!* Then, not being one to offer any help, he plods off.

I had no rope, no grain for bribery purposes, but figured the girls would come when I called. At least, I hoped so.
I found the broken section of electric fence, gritted my teeth
and checked it. No current. No wonder. When I located the
cows, Madame had them penned in a corner of a field and
was holding them there with the aid of a big German shepherd which barked menacingly from time to time. I carefully
moved toward them and called out. Like well-behaved children they formed a line and followed me. Right up to the dog,
which barked and sent them scrambling back to the corner. I
tried again with the same results. I asked Madame to take the
dog home, but she mumbled, "My husband insists I stay until
the cows are gone." My pleas about the dog fell on deaf ears.
"Mon mari m'a dit." Her lord spake.

I asked to borrow a rope. She shrugged. This was no
time to tarry. I told myself my cotton bra was not revealing
and it was only us girls anyway. (I'm not sure about the dog.)
So I tugged off my tee shirt, wrapped it around Olga's neck
and led the girls right out of the lion's den and back home.
But after I was back in my own field and the fence put back
together, I looked across to see Madame still standing there,
her hand on the dog, her mouth open wide.

I'm so proud of how well the children are doing in
school. In spite of having to learn a new language right along
with history, math, geography and other subjects, not one of
them has fallen back or missed a beat. One of their teachers
told me it is primarily because of their basic abilities and
grounding in mathematics (which is a language unto itself). I
credit hard work. Now they look and sound just like the local
kids. Wendy, Danny and Tim have all recovered from the tonsils' episode but Jill, who felt so left out at the time, just had

her turn. Only it wasn't her tonsils that were infected, but her appendix. We had an awful night, with her throwing up at hourly intervals until by the time the sun came up at 6:00 A.M., I figured it was high time the doctor got involved.

Dr. DeJean, our village doctor, lives a different life from physicians in the States. He isn't safe from his patients when he's at home, because his office is the downstairs floor of his home, right on the main street. We threw on jeans and tee shirts and headed downtown while I prayed Jill wouldn't throw up in the car on the way.

At 6:00 A.M., the village is pretty quiet and deserted. The doctor's doorbell pealed out like a church chime. Nevertheless, it took several rings before his tousled head poked out an upstairs window and growled, *"Mon Dieu!* Do you have any idea what time it is? Come back at eight like civilized folk."

Just before the window slammed shut, Jill took appropriate action and threw up all over his door mat.

"Ça va! Ça va! Attendez un minute."

I felt badly when he told us that he'd been up all night delivering a baby.

After a few tests, he sent us on our way to the hospital in Perigueux, about one hundred miles away. Jill's ready-to-burst appendix was whipped out before nightfall. After a few days of special care, Jill was fine.

Dr. DeJean told me later that his door mat was a total loss. I don't believe that's covered under the *Securité Sociale*, which is the national health insurance.

Speaking of health, I have been trying to learn about the local mushrooms so I won't poison the entire family with a new delicacy at the dinner table. When our neighbors, the

Saint-Martins, invited me to join an expedition with a mushroom expert into the woods to identify the various species, I
decided I'd better go. The children and I can't take any more
health emergencies.

I'd been told that no poison varieties grow in the open
fields, that only the dark woods breed the deadly types.
Therefore, I'd been plucking the little *nez de chat* (cat's nose)
mushrooms (if I could get to them before the cows did)
which grow in rings in the fields. I was becoming convinced
that if I could just get there early in the morning when the
dew was still shimmering, I might see a fairy wing disappear
underneath the cap.

The mushroom expert, the group and I slogged
around in the soggy underbrush, peeking under leaves and
moss, collecting one of each of everything we could find and
then gathered in a relatively dry clearing to compare the little
gems. I never knew how many different kinds there were, but
according to our guide, we'd barely scratched the surface.
Nor did I ever appreciate them as gourmet delicacies, until I
tasted them in France, lightly grilled with garlic and herbs or
braised in butter until just crispy.

We found orange *girolles*, huge *cèpes* like pancakes-on-
a-stem and pock-marked *morilles*. Our expert showed us pictures of the *trompette des morts,* which he swore was excellent, but with that name I doubt I could ever trust it.

One of our group found one which is instantly fatal
and our guide became very excited and tried to explain how
the little ridge on the stem differed from the little ridges on
the stems of the tasty varieties. They all looked the same to
me. I decided I was going to stick to the ones I gathered in the
open fields and those I could buy in the market.

As the mushroom-hunting group relaxed and gossiped with each other, I learned that the entire village was in an uproar. Sports and politics had mixed it up big time the night before. As I understand it, it went something like this. One of the mayoral candidates was a big rugby fan, his son being one of the team stars. The other candidate was a supporter of the trotting races, which were also very popular here, with the Sunday *tiercé* the most hotly debated issue after the weather.

Saint-Cyprien has a large field on the edge of the village with a track around the outer edge for the trotters and turf in the middle for rugby matches. Races were scheduled for this coming Sunday. During the night, someone (rumor has it that it was those rascally rugby-ers) plowed the entire field, including the track, making it unfit for the horses. As I said, the village was in an uproar with words and fists flying. I decided it was time to go home to my peaceful hillside, which is what I did.

And now it's time to pick up the kids at school and I haven't halfway finished the day's chores. The fence line presents a constant problem as I try to maintain a strong current throughout. All it takes is for the wire to touch a weed or a tree to short out the rest of the line and the way weeds grow around here I need to make cutting expeditions almost daily.

And it's amazing how quickly the cows cotton on to an electricity outage. They seem to have a sixth sense for current pulsing through the wires and within a day of no pulses, they're out.

Much love from all of us to all of you,

Jan

PS: Our neighbor, M'sieur Saint-Martin, is also a bit of a local history buff and last week peered into the barns at *Vezat* and confirmed the presence of large rocks placed at the base of the structure and found only in the river bed. These rocks were long believed to bring fertility to the land, fecundity to the beasts and health and prosperity to the farmers. The rocks themselves were humongous and had been hauled up from the river bottom some time in the seventeenth century, long before mechanized means of transport. Some poor ox pulled a mighty heavy load!

❦ CHAPTER 32 ❧

A Christmas Gift

The years were passing, each with its own trove of memories. The holidays always added more. Once again, it was Christmas morning and the sun shone intermittently between grey forbidding clouds and the frozen ground crunched underfoot.

The Christmas tree in the kitchen stood in the middle of bright wrappings, crinkled and tossed into torn scraps, and gift boxes neatly stacked. Tree ornaments reflected the colored lights shining in a valiant attempt to bring brightness into the dismal day. Two cats, a calico and a big orange, stretched out luxuriously on top of the single space heater, the only spot close enough to feel any warmth. The rest of the family gathered around the breakfast table, devouring eggs, bacon and French toast (don't kid yourself, the French never heard of it) and warming their hands with mugs of hot chocolate. I had my hands firmly gripped around a cup of *café au lait*, which I consider to be the major humanitarian invention of France, trying to ward off chilblains from an hour spent milking in the open barn with an east wind blowing through. That morning, even the cows had icicles growing on their horns and chins.

The three dogs surrounded the table, six eyes never leaving the children's hands, waiting for something, anything to drop. If it weren't for all the muddy feet, our kitchen floor would be the cleanest in town. No food ever touched it.

Gabriel burst in like Santa himself, ho-ho-ho-ing and stomping his feet, only instead of a bag of goodies he carried a tiny lamb so dirty and smelly as to be practically unrecognizable. The dogs surrounded him with barks of greeting, jumping up to smell this strange, odoriferous creature.

"My brother's wife put this little one on the manure pile, said it was as good as dead. The ewe died giving birth. Brought it to you, you'll fix him up right as rain." And before I knew what he was doing, the tiny creature was in my arms. "*Joyeux Noël, les enfants!*"

First order of business was getting Gabriel some coffee. His had the addition of some *eau de vie*, a form of antifreeze guaranteed to re-start the blood flow. *Eau de vie* literally translates to "water of life," but in actuality, it is more akin to "instant death." It's a clear liqueur made from plums, and heartily enjoyed by all the local farmers, who drink it in straight shots or liberally mixed in their coffee. Their wives consume it on sugar lumps, placed on a spoon and dipped into the stuff.

Gabriel, mug firmly in hand, leaned on the heater nearly sitting on the cats, who weren't about to give up their prime spots, while I rounded up old towels and a cardboard box to make a warm nest for the infant. I wrapped him up snugly in the towels and placed him in the box pushed up close beside the heater. I couldn't feel much life in the little body.

While I boiled rice to create the rice water necessary to stop diarrhea, the kids discussed names for this latest addition to the household. As I scrounged in back cupboards for a baby bottle and nipple which hadn't been destroyed by the last baby calf, they debated Rudolph and Frosty, but as I blended just a taste of powdered milk into the rice water mix, they settled unanimously on Nicholas, Nicky for short.

I held the little guy on my lap, still wrapped firmly in a warm towel, and popped the bottle into his mouth. His eyes weren't even open and I feared he was too far gone. I shook the bottle lightly and a few drops of the warm mixture fell on his tongue. He mouthed the nipple and pulled out more, just a taste, then the eyes opened in surprise and he sucked, strong and steady.

"I knew it, told you so. You can do anything with the little beasts." Gabriel's smile was as wide as his face as he refilled his mug with *eau de vie* and added a drop of coffee to warm it up. The lamb slept happily in his nest by the heater, his tummy full and warm, mouthing drops of milk in his sleep.

The next few weeks were filled with bottle feedings every four hours, day and night. I really thought this sort of schedule had departed with the growth of my youngest child. Silly me. The first sunny day after the departure of the diarrhea, I risked bathing the little guy. I used the kitchen sink, just as I would with any infant. Big mistake.

Two hours later I had a clean, fluffy black and white spotted lamb, a clean kitchen counter and a clean kitchen floor. As for me, I was splattered from head to foot with dirty water liberally mixed with bits of wool and totally exhausted. The dogs and cats abandoned the kitchen early in the process, along with the deterioration of my good disposition, but Nicky was now happy and frisky.

The boys were enchanted with their new game of pushing on Nicky's brow which caused the feisty little animal to butt determinedly against their hands. The drawback surfaced the day I was standing at the sink and suddenly the backs of my knees were attacked and I was on the floor with a small black and white creature backing up to make another run. We anxiously watched the weather for signs of warming so that Nicky could be moved out to the pen with the bigger sheep.

The few glimmers of sun had departed and winter returned in earnest, bringing with it freezing rains by day, and night, which turned the dripping trees to frozen gargoyles. Only the needs of the livestock persuaded any of us to set foot outdoors. Ice formed several inches deep on the water in the aluminum reservoir used by the cows and needed to be broken up at regular intervals. We piled fresh straw into the rabbit hutches. The little creatures were protected from the constant drizzle by the barn overhang, but fingers of freezing wind reached every cranny and crevice. Their water bowls froze solid and could only be thawed by the addition of warm water, then re-froze within the hour. The cows foraged in the woods, ever hopeful of finding one last green and tender shoot under the carpeting of leaves and pine needles. By mid-afternoon, sodden and with ice forming on their horns and eyelashes, they retreated to the comparative shelter of the open milking barn. There, they found fresh, dry straw and could chew their cuds in contemplative peace until their suppers of fresh hay and cracked corn appeared.

One bitter cold evening after dinner and clean-up, we all crowded around the heater, draped with its usual contingent of cats, drawing what warmth we could from it and from each other. Nicky was amusing himself butting the kitchen cabinets when one of the doors popped open under the force of the blow and a bottle of ammonia fell to the floor and smashed. The pungent fumes filled the room and with eyes streaming, dogs, cats, humans and lamb headed for the outside and the freezing—and un-ammoniated—air.

It quickly became clear that if we were ever again to inhabit the kitchen, heart of our home and only source of heat, someone had to clean up the ammonia. Guess who? When Nicky had turned into a juvenile delinquent, he quickly became MY lamb and, of course, at moments like this, Gabriel was nowhere near. I grabbed a lungful of fresh air, dashed inside, deposited broken bottle bits in a bag and mixed a sinkful of hot sudsy water for soaking up the ammonia. All of this was accomplished in intermittent bursts, each lasting as long as a lungful of air, at which time I dashed back outside to be greeted with barks, meows and:

"You nearly done?"

"What's taking so long?"

"Hey, it's cold out here!"

"Mom, can't you hurry!"

"Baa! Baa!"

accompanied by stamping feet, hand clapping and head butting. When I suggested that the job would go faster with more hands, a deep silence followed. Even the head butter wandered off.

The most eager of the group streaming back into the comparative warmth of the kitchen was Nicky, who pressed his body directly against the heater until we smelled burning wool and had to pry him off, wrap him in a warm towel and tuck him back into his box to fall into the deep sleep of the innocent.

↭ CHAPTER 33 ↭

Deadly Drought

"*Merde!*" As the years passed, my language was acquiring a lot of local color. Particularly in my own milking barn surrounded only by cows who were equally as cranky. And with good reason. Drought. One hell of a good reason.

The whole year hadn't gone well. Starting with the second hour of the first day of the new year. Returning home from a New Year's Eve *reveillon* with Jane and René, who were dearer to us now than blood kin and certainly geographically closer, we were greeted by a frozen geyser arching out and down the side of the building. It sparkled back at the moon and stars in the clear, cold sky like an ice sculpture.

"Ooooh, Mom, it's beautiful," Jill breathed, fearful that it would shatter and disappear.

I wished it would. It was way too late at night, actually too early in the morning, and I had consumed far too much wine to even consider trouble-shooting the situation at that moment. Oysters are a traditional treat for the year-end fêtes.

While I can't quite manage oysters—in fact, I gag—we had discovered a white wine...dry, nutty, a hint of spice. It was delicious. I handed my oysters to René and he kept my wine glass filled the rest of the evening.

I was glad to be home. Before wishing the children a happy New Year and good night, I had sufficient good sense to turn off the main water line. Collapsing into bed, I was soon asleep, with visions of oysters and ice columns dancing in my dreams.

Rob was still part of the children's lives on a once-a-year basis. During his annual visit the previous summer, he had floored a portion of the attic over the kitchen to make a room for Danny, as well as a small second bathroom, this one with a real tub. New Year's morning, we discovered that the broken water line was the hot water pipe, lying without insulation along the eaves leading to this bathroom. For the next few weeks, we resumed operations with cold water only. Repairs of this nature in our area of France, where running water of any sort is a luxury, are not considered "emergency" and are handled in due course. Like next spring, maybe. For now, cold showers.

The remaining winter days were short and often grey, but lacked the deep freeze and bone-aching cold of past years. In February, we received the gift of a few perfect weeks, hinting at spring to come, where the sun shone from a clear blue sky and the winter plowing was done wearing light sweaters and feeling the sheer joy of being alive. The plum and apple trees bordering the lane had already burst into joyous bloom.

In March, our evil genie struck again. One morning we awoke to a heavy frost covering the hillside with a million sparkling crystals and turning every spiderweb into a tapestry of shimmering lace. The children, including the older two, grabbed their "flying saucers," round-bottomed plastic skimmers, and raced up the sloping fields to come flying back down again. The cattle appeared for morning milking with icicles attached to their horns and dangling in front of their eyes. All the tender new fruit buds blackened and died.

We had grown careless with the mildness of the winter and had left the water hose out in the courtyard. Needless to say, it was frozen solid and it wasn't until nearly noon, when it had lain in the sun for several hours, that I was able to shoot out long round popsicles of ice and, finally, a stream of water. The water container for the cattle that stood in the field was fortunately at least half full and we were able to break up the deep covering of ice with the shovel.

The spring months which followed were lovely. The trees greened as did the fields, but it wasn't long before the lack of rains from the fall and winter began to be noticed in the delayed growth of the hay crop. The corn and barley crops were slow to germinate and, when they did, it was only a sparse coverage on the fields. Those farmers who had fields in the valley of the Dordogne River ran irrigation from the river and had long pipes and sprinkler mechanisms. We on the hillside listened to the sound of their sprinklers every evening and prayed for rain.

The alfalfa crop was too sparse to have any hope of a harvest and there was so little other growing feed for the cattle that I turned them into the field, fencing off bit by precious bit, making it last as long as possible. I started asking around, offering to cut hay at other farms in return for half of the crop for myself.

Through the grapevine, I heard of a widow with a farm in the hills above Le Coux, close to an hour away by trac- tor. She had a couple of cows and needed only part of her hay and was willing to split it with someone who would do all the work. Through my grapevine contact, she accepted my ser- vices.

"Eh oui, pauvre femme." René, of course, knew all about the widow. It seemed, he told me, that after she was widowed some ten years ago, she had hired two transient workers and allowed them to live in her home. They milked her cows and took care of farm chores. She was in her eight- ies and they were each close to seventy and vowed that if she didn't leave them the property in her will, they would burn it to the ground.

"Alors, sûrtout, ne mangez pas chez elle! Make any excuse, but don't eat with them." René made no further expla- nation.

After driving through back country roads on the trac- tor to cut the hay, I didn't meet the widow, but one of her hired hands met me at the road. Tall, dark and thin, he touched one hand briefly to his beret as I chugged up and pointed to a field hidden in dense foliage and scrub pines. Then, without a word, he strode off.

I drove down a narrow lane and emerged at a field with a dense weedy growth. This field didn't appear to have suffered a lack of rain and as I walked through I discovered why. A hidden, totally overgrown creek flowed through the center. *Putain de merde!*

During the next few hours I had the opportunity of bringing out every morsel of vocabulary I'd learned over the past years as I sweated and struggled to cut the sticky weeds and avoid falling in the creek. The growth at the water's edge had a distinct smell of anise, there was an occasional stalk of alfalfa mixed in with the rest, but overall the hay was nowhere near the quality my girls had come to expect. I hoped it would fill their stomachs.

I gave the hay a couple days to dry before raking, but even then it was so dense and shaded that it lopped over in damp matted piles. Monsieur Lariviere, the entrepreneur with the baling machine, was going to hate me for this job. *"L'Americaine! Quelle idiote!"* I could hear it now.

My son Tim and I set out right after milking to collect the hay, delivering one load to the widow and bringing the second home. I hoped one or both of the handymen would give us a hand, but neither was waiting at the field and we piled the bales onto the *remorque* alone. I kept the tractor with its heavy load well away from the creek.

This was my first sight of the farm itself and of the widow as we pulled into the courtyard. It was easy to see why she needed help. She was a tiny wisp of a woman with a brown, wizened face, wearing a long-sleeved high-necked cotton dress with heavy work shoes and a bonnet straight out of pioneer days. I approached to greet her, but was immediately face to face with the same dark, taciturn man I'd seen before and a second man who was the spitting image of Frankenstein. Square face, flat top, scar on cheek, close to seven feet tall, even walked with a limp. He thrust a heavily veined hand first at me then at Tim. I couldn't look at Tim; I knew I'd giggle.

No one spoke, obviously conversationally-challenged, but the dark man pointed toward the barn and Frankenstein jogged over to it, disappeared inside and reappeared at a small attic window. If he was planning to help, we'd make short work of this load, but as I backed into position, he motioned to Tim, "You come."

While I forked up the bales, he pointed to indicate the appropriate placement for Tim. The other man stayed below, arms folded, keeping a close eye on me. God knows what damage we could do while unloading a trailer full of hay, but they were keeping careful watch on us.

It was hot work in the airless attic, particularly for Tim. When we finished, sweat rolled off us both. We stashed the pitchforks and jumped down, requesting water, and the dark man pointed to a hose in the courtyard. Under his shocked gaze, we not only drank deeply but poured the cool liquid over our heads and necks. The first time Gabriel saw me do that he assured me that cold water on the head would cause brain damage and I laughingly replied that it was already too late. I began to think that might not be a joke.

Turning off the water I saw a group of rabbit hutches and walked over. There were several fat rabbits and a couple of litters of infants and...a big yellow cat. He blinked amber eyes, but didn't move. I turned to Madame, who had walked out beside me, and asked if he were injured.

"No, he's been there for three years, ever since he tried to run away."

I'll bet they'd never catch him if he got out again.

Madame asked if we'd like some lunch before return- ing for the second load and I hesitated, smelling warm garlic and spices coming from the kitchen. Then, remembering René's warning, I thanked her and said our time was limited and we needed to hurry. At that moment, we saw Frankenstein emerging from the kitchen with a large country ham tucked under his arm, already undoing the buttons on his *bleue de travail* as he headed around the side of the barn to *pisser*. He must have been slicing it when the urge struck.

Tim and I headed for the tractor calling back *"Merci"* and were out the lane and back into the shady, weedy field before we collapsed on the ground laughing. We got up and ran down to the little stream and splashed water on our faces. Then we made quick work of the second load and headed for home, munching on some bread and cheese I'd stashed on the tractor.

As I backed into the big double doors of our barn, René and Jane were waiting for us to help unload the hay. Now, THAT I was proud of, being able to back a *remorque* loaded with hay into the opening without destroying either of the big doors. Of course, it took a long time to learn. Both boys did it on their first try and they could barely reach the pedals. Little show-offs!

"Mais, c'est de la merde, ça." René was fingering and smelling the hay distastefully. Unfortunately, when it came time for the cows to eat it, they were in total agreement.

By late June the usually plush greenery of the fields, which should have been ankle-high after a May cutting, was brown and stubbly like a two-day old growth of beard. The ground was cracked and dry. The heat rose to new highs every day.

The cows spent more time in the shady woods and any leaf low enough to be snatched into a questing mouth had long since been chewed and re-chewed. Cows enjoy their food more than once, you know.

The pond around the spring which provided our water had been dropping and I'd been monitoring our use pretty carefully. Still, when the water dribbled a drop or two from the hose then stopped, I set it down with irritation to look for the kink. No kink.

"Dan! Tim! Would one of you please prime the pump? The dang water has stopped again." This happened once or twice a day now and interrupting chores to prime the pump was a major pain south of the beltline.

"Mom! C'mere. You gotta see this!" Danny's voice rang clearly up the hill. I had a feeling that I didn't really want to see, but knew there was no way of avoiding it. For the past years we'd faced every problem hurled at us and always got past. We didn't always win or even come out ahead, but we did get by. I had a gut instinct another one was coming. A biggie.

The pond, which had always stood around the old oak, bubbling in the center from a steady surge of underground water, was gone. Formerly dark green, the watercress around the edges lay limp and brown. The pump sucked and gasped until I took pity on its useless labors and turned it off.

When we first moved onto the farm, we had no running water but at least we had a source from which to fill buckets. For five human beings, two dogs and a pair of cats. Now we were the same number of humans, three dogs, heaven-knows-how-many cats, eight cows, six calves, a bunch of bunnies, a gaggle of chickens and probably a few miscellaneous whatevers that I'd neglected to tally. And no water at all. Dear God, please let this be a passing trial, I prayed.

I hopped in the car and headed up to *Saint Pompon*. I needed both of my friends, Jane for sympathy and René for advice. As always, they both came through.

Jane set the tea kettle on to boil and René stuck a glass of wine in my hand. *"Eh oui. Ça arrive.* You'll need a tonneau, *une tonne*, to haul water. You go see what you can find and I'll talk to *le Parisien* across the road. They have a summer place with a deep well, I'm sure they'll let you have some."

I headed down to the local tractor dealer and repairman. My tractor was old and secondhand, but he kept it running for me, as well as finding used equipment at relatively decent prices. I liked him because he treated me fairly, never asked me to send my husband to discuss business matters and probably cheated me no worse than any of the other farmers. Besides, he made a conscious effort to keep his language clean when talking with me.

He nodded sagely when I told him my problem and assured me that I wasn't the first who was suffering. And wouldn't be the last. Most of the farms on the hill were being hit. He motioned to the sprinklers re-cycling water from the river through miles of pipes across fields of corn and tobacco. They were the lucky ones. *"Eh oui."*

I was in luck. He had one used *tonne* left. I signed the paper which added this to my current bill. Most of the local farmers paid their bills when the tobacco crop sold. I paid mine when my annual crop of calves sold. Some of the calves were the offspring of my own cows, others I bought as five-day-old infants from neighboring farms. Raising them was a labor of love and when I sold them it was to be bred and kept as milk cows, not to be chopped up for hamburger. Rather like a foster parent turning out a contributing new member of society. Only I got paid for it.

I drove home to collect the tractor and return for my new acquisition. The tractor man suggested I fill it up at the river and directed me to a spot where I could use a hose attached to the sprinkler system. When I pulled into the courtyard with the *tonne* filled with water, the cows were chorusing *"Meuh"* over the nearly empty *bac* at the edge of the field.

The *tonne* required filling twice a day to supply water needs for the animals, ourselves, washing and bathing. No matter what other chores were scheduled for the day, the *rateau, remorque,* plow or whatever was removed from the tractor morning and evening and the *tonne* attached for the water run. The cows were the major wage earners for the farm and under no circumstances must they ever be allowed to be water-deprived. They didn't hesitate to remind me of that fact if I let their *bac* run low.

The Parisian had shown René how to operate his pump and assured him they were delighted to be able to help. His family would be down for the summer the following week, but there was water to spare in the deep well. The property was close enough that I could make the round trip, including fill-time, in half an hour. This wasn't going to be so bad after all!

That is, until the Parisian's family arrived. Madame *la Parisienne* was outside as I drove up and waved. She was tall and slender, coiffed, perfumed, mascara'd and dressed for a day in the country with white form-fitting slacks, a bright yellow shirt tied fashionably at the waist, *très décolletée,* and strappy sandals with three-inch heels. She watched as I filled the *tonne*, but disappeared into the house when I drove out.

"Je suis désolée." She blocked the road on my next tour, then came around to speak with me, staying well clear of my dirty tractor and any possible exhaust fumes. She didn't look desolated. "We have need of the water. You must find another source."

In front of the house a lawn sprinkler sent vast quantities of water spiraling into the air and two small children dashed screaming in and out of the stream. The water jetting into the air would have filled a small wading pool ten times over as I watched.

"Les enfants, vous savez...perhaps the river," she gestured scarlet manicured fingertips vaguely in the direction of the Dordogne.

I thanked her—I'm not sure for what—and turned the tractor and *tonne* around, heading for the spot on the river I'd used before. The distance meant more than an hour for the round trip. Twice a day.

Fortunately, another friend offered to share a water supply. It's times like these when friends stand up for counting. This source was toward the village, farther than the Parisians but closer than the river. I needed to carry a length of hose, but there was a spigot. The following week, it gave the familiar burp, spit out a couple of drops and quit. *Merde!* Back to the river.

Days, weeks, months. Time was endless, hot, dusty, arid. Nothing grew. Green was a remembered color. My life was spent on the tractor, driving to water or away from water, hooking up the *tonne,* unhooking the *tonne.* I counted the bales in the too-slowly growing pile in the barn and carefully measured the grain left from the year before. The stunted corn was cut green in the field and fed in great armfuls to the hungry cows.

The math wasn't working. No matter how many times I tried, the number of cows on our farm wouldn't divide into the number of bales of hay and come out with a number equal to the days before the next crop. And that was assuming that rain would fall, filling the great gaping cracks in the fields and bringing life back to the parched grasses.

Facing facts can be truly difficult. I knew I wasn't a good farmer. Good farmers don't give pet names to every beast on their farm and turn vegetarian rather than slaughter any of them. Good farmers can sell livestock when the situation requires without feeling like they are selling their children.

Still, I now knew I had to do it. I had to sell two of the ladies of the herd. There was, quite simply, not enough feed for all. What made it even worse, the only buyer was *l'abattoir*, the slaughter house. No other dairy farmer was buying cows during this time, in fact, they were facing the same dire circumstances I was.

Gritting my teeth and hardening my heart, I selected Petula and Lily, the two with the lowest milk production. This, in spite of the fact that Lily was a beautiful red and white Normandy cow which I had raised from a calf. She was sweet-tempered and gentle and came when I called her for a head scratch. I resolutely wiped away the tears and drove down to *l'abattoire* and made the deal. The following day the truck arrived, driven by a pimply-faced young man whom I hated on sight.

I stood miserably by as he went in the barn to get Petula, but when she balked at stepping up the loading ramp and he goosed her with a high voltage cattle prod, I ran over and smacked his hand away, yelling, *"Sadist dégoûtant!"* He stepped back and looked amazed at my reaction to such a normal practice in his business. Instead I coaxed both girls up the ramp and attached them in the trailer. Then I patted the two soft necks, backed out, waved the driver out the lane and, through a haze of tears, stood looking down at the herd grazing in the field below.

Selling my children by the pound gave me no sense of pride, no satisfaction over a successful business transaction. Love the job as I might, I'd never make a farmer.

❧ PART 3 ❧

La Bonne Vie

The brown calloused fingers gripped
the secateurs delicately, deftly.
The broad hand was stained with soil, with
fruits of forgotten harvests, grease
from derelict tractors.
An old scar on the right back from
the left rear of a cranky bull.

The vineyard rows stretched long and straight,
like an army of misshapen gnomes
awaiting the sorcerer's return.
He snipped old growth with the precision
of a surgeon,
lovingly, reverently.

"Why," I asked. "Why such tender care? It's just
old growth, old vines."
He stopped, shifted the secateurs to the other hand and
flexed his fingers. His eyes, round with wonder,
gazed into mine.
He shook his head.
"Good wine," he responded, "truly great wine comes
only with loving care from the day of its birth.
Like children."

❧ CHAPTER 34 ❧

More Than a Shower

"*C'est que de la politique, ça!*" Gabriel slapped his right hand on his left upper arm, raising his left hand in a very rude gesture as he blamed the politicians once again for not helping farmers like him profit from the land on which they worked so hard. The hill farmers, having no means of watering their crops, had watched sadly while the corn and rye wilted, but had quickly turned in their claims when the tobacco turned brown. Only a month before he'd been ecstatic when the insurance company paid him for his tobacco crop lying dead in the field from a lack of water.

The jubilation died when he and other farmers who depended on nature realized that prices for the crops thriving in the valley with regular irrigation from river water were predicted to reach new highs. According to Gabriel, *les salauds* in the government ranked right down with *les sales capitalistes* in the insurance companies. I kept a low profile.

My only problem with the river farmers lay in their increasing efforts to make it more difficult for the rest of us to draw water. Though the Dordogne was public, they closed every access road possible and removed the handles and spigots from their pipes, requiring us to dip the water bucket by bucket.

August turned to September. There was no second hay cutting. The alfalfa, which should have been thigh-high, had straggled only to the height of a child's ankle and was colored the palest green. I turned the cows into the field, giving them a few inches each day of the precious feed. At night, they were finishing up the last of the corn, cut green on the stalk.

The sky was the color of oatmeal, flecks of darker clouds lumped into the creamy haze. Far-off thunder rumbled as if the gods were suffering digestive distress. I moved with the speed and grace of a bear mucking through a swamp and felt about as lovable.

Bathing was done with half a bucket of water, if we were lucky. Swimming in the river was no longer an option; it was too muddy to improve the situation. I was beginning to wonder if it was worth the effort. Every time I cleaned up, some cow just swatted me with a tail covered in smelly, unmentionable stuff. How they could turn dry fodder into *that* was beyond me.

I finished up the evening milking as the sky grew steadily darker and rumbled louder. Even the cats were nervous. Fanny, my favorite, normally perched happily on my shoulder during the entire process, purring and drooling down my shirt, but now she was up and down and pacing just out of reach of the hoof of a cranky cow. Two big yellow males squabbled over a shallow cookie tin into which I had splashed some warm milk.

Olga was about the only cow that was unfailingly calm and even-tempered. After I hooked up the milking machine and settled back on my three-legged stool, she paused in her munching to reach back and run a sandpaper tongue up my back, raising my shirt. Hot tears spurted in my eyes as I thought about Petula and Lily.

"Oh, Olga, if you only knew. You'd never love me again."

Tears were never far behind my eyes these days. It took little or nothing to set me off. It might have been the fatigue from the incessant water runs. It might have been the heat, the oppressive air, the growling in the sky. I think mostly it was sheer despair.

These days everyone walked with head down, shoulders a little bent. I hadn't heard Gabriel's irrepressible chuckle in weeks. *L'oncle* was thinking of selling all three of his cows and retiring with his *Securité Sociale*. Jane and René had sold nearly a third of their flock of sheep, along with several of their special pets. The hay harvests had provided little to celebrate and we hadn't had a *fête de foin* all summer. Actually, we'd tried to have one, for old time's sake, but it turned into a wake. And that was, sure as hell, no fun at all.

Some days I fantasized about selling off the whole works, farm and all, admitting defeat, tucking my tail between my legs and heading back to the States. My parents had died several years before we left, but Rob's family, whom I loved dearly, wanted us to come back. They were never very comfortable with our venture on "foreign soil." I think they were always a little suspicious of people who didn't speak English.

But damn! I didn't want to admit defeat. If I quit, I wanted it to be when I chose, when I was ahead. I needed to prove something—mostly to myself.

Dinner that night was argumentative and messy. I fixed spaghetti, which was cheap, easy and usually liked by all. With four kids, there aren't too many items which fit those requirements. However, there was as much growling around the table as there was in the sky. Milk was spilled, landing on a cat importunately sitting under the table's edge. He retired in high dudgeon to clean himself and scowl at the culprits. Jerry walked beside the table and swiped his huge tail over a plate of spaghetti, sending the plate upside down and a spray of sauce across Jill's shirt.

Tears were wiped, another (the last) clean shirt found, pets fed and patted, the television turned on and water was heating for dishes when I realized the sky had turned totally black and the wind was sending empty buckets flying through the courtyard. The rumbling ceased, then a crack sounded as if shot from a gun. Lights and TV went out. Adult, children and animals all gravitated into a tiny spot dead center in the room, as if together we could withstand whatever was about to commence.

Splat! Splat! Splat!

"Mom, it's raining." Danny's voice was hushed, almost reverent.

We ran to the window. It was. The drops continued, then were no longer drops. A solid sheet of water descended. It was as if Someone up there suddenly realized, *Oops, forgot to water earth*. And turned on the hose.

Thank you, God. Oh, thank you thank you thank you.

We couldn't even see the barn across the courtyard through the wall of water. It rained. It poured. It immersed. I stripped off my grubby shorts and shirt right down to skin and grabbed a bar of soap off the kitchen sink.

"Race you to the shower," I yelled as I stepped out the door into the waterfall.

"But, Mom, what if someone comes?" a small shocked voice queried.

"In this deluge?" I called back.

The boys and dogs didn't take long to follow and we danced like idiots, passing around the soap and lathering off what seemed like weeks, like months of accumulated sweat and grime. I stuck my hand in the door and requested that Jill hand me the shampoo, which she did with obvious disapproval. I guess not everyone's mother danced naked in the rain. On the other hand, Jill hadn't spent as much time as I had with the cows.

"It's raining, it's pouring, the old man is snoring."

We danced and sang. We lathered each other's heads. Then we lathered the dogs. In no time, the rain rinsed all of us. We glowed. We sparkled. We were so clean we squeaked.

The biggest thing to remember about farming isn't the work. It isn't the equipment. It's not even the animals. It's the fact that you can't do it all. It's a partnership. You do what you can, you labor with every muscle and bone in your body, with every brain cell you can muster. You get advice from experts. But you can't control the weather. Drought, flood, hurricane, tornado. Your Supreme Partner needs to do His part. And He never shares with you His overall plans. In other words, if you're a human being without divine sight, life's a crapshoot.

I still loved ours. And we weren't beaten yet. There was hope springing to life. *Eh oui.* Thank you thank you thank you.

CHAPTER 35

Selling Livestock

Our drought healed itself fairly rapidly. A fall of drenching rains, a winter of more of the same along with some snow and the springs bubbled again. Green sprouted everywhere, even between the rocks in the buildings.

I was left with one little problem, that is, two little problems. Two calves out of my herd of youngsters, who had been about six months old during the height of the summer heat and who had decided between themselves that it was too hot to hike to the *bac* for a drink, had laid down in the woods and dehydrated. Just plumb dried out. I discovered them missing at suppertime when I took armloads of green cornstalks out to augment the sparse pickings in the pasture.

A search of the woods soon revealed the girls lying weak and panting on the packed dirt, where even the dried leaves had long since been scarfed down. They didn't look at all well.

The veterinarian was rapidly acquiring the status of a family member. I certainly spent more francs on Dr. Marchaud than on all the kids combined. This time he came up right away, *tout de suite,* gave each animal a shot of something, told me to keep the calves in a barn and put them back on a dilute milk mixture. He said praying wouldn't hurt either.

The calves had obviously decided to die and they weren't about to get up and move around under their own steam. With the help of the boys, I got out an old blanket and, one at a time, rolled the girls onto it and dragged them into the barn. After all that effort and expense, I wasn't ready to let the calves give up. After a night and a day of plying the sick creatures with water mixed with milk powder and handfuls of precious grain, they finally scrambled to their feet and set about the process of coming back to life. Sometimes nagging pays off.

It wasn't long before they rejoined their sisters, but their growth had taken a major setback and they didn't develop like the others. They didn't act like the others either, following me around like big dogs, nuzzling my hands and pockets for treats. Spoiling, for any species, is easily learned but unlearned only with great difficulty. Sometimes never.

By winter, after the rains were showing signs of repairing the intensive damage of the drought, regional farmers started buying young animals to build up their herds. I wasn't the only one who'd had to sell off livestock. My yearlings, except for the two runts, sold quickly and well. Those two I hid in the barn when showing the others. They were going to require a lot more time and effort and they certainly wouldn't do much for my reputation for raising healthy calves.

The French government, bless their sweet generous socialistic hearts, decided some disaster relief was in order and started handing out money to any farmer who had lost crops and livestock. The relief was based on the number of hectares under cultivation for grains as well as those in pasture and the number of animals in the herds. In addition to outright payments, farmers could borrow money for livestock or equipment at an unheard of interest rate of 4 percent. Manna from heaven. Even I, as a property owner, was eligible.

I bought a couple of young cows that would be calving within the month to build up the milking herd and acquired another half dozen babies. The two spoiled yearlings took almost a maternal interest in the little ones and after they were old enough to leave the barn for the fields, shepherded them around solicitously. The babies thrived on lush grasses and a bountiful crop of rye and when they became yearlings they were indeed plump and well-formed. The runts, now two years old, were also chubby, glossy-coated and seemed scarcely older than the others.

As I spread the word that the calves were available for sale, many spirited discussions took place between the golden lady with wings and a halo on my right shoulder and the pointy-horned guy on the left.

"But that's dishonest!" (wings)

"So? All's fair in love and livestock." (pointy-horns)

"Think of ethics, of honor. Think Golden Rule." (wings)

"I say, think about doing to others what's been done to us. We've been cheated at every opportunity for years. And what's the harm?" (pointy-horns)

And I let that little devil win. I sold the two-year old runts as if they were exceedingly well-developed yearlings to a little old couple who were as excited about them as if they were adopting a pair of children. They requested I deliver the calves to their small farm near Le Coux, twenty-five miles out the river road. With a guilty conscience, I agreed to borrow a stock trailer and bring them the following morning.

I realized a nice sum on the sale, although after tallying veterinarian bills and two years of feeding, there was probably a net loss on the transaction. But—there was guilt! BIG guilt!

My neighbor up the hill, M'sieur Gorse, loaned me his double trailer and I started out right after milking and taking the kids to school. With the speed of my tractor pulling the loaded trailer, twenty-five miles was over an hour run. We arrived just before noon.

The old couple was waiting, and we escorted the girls into a barn loaded with fresh sweet straw and piles of alfalfa hay. Two elderly cows surveyed the proceedings with a great deal of interest.

"You'll stay for lunch, *bien sûr*," the wife said, tucking a few stray hairs into her bun.

"Oh no, *merci*. I really must get back." All I wanted to do was get out of there. Before I broke down and admitted my evil deed.

Her husband shook his head. *"Bien sûr que non!"*

They wouldn't hear of my leaving and with as much grace as I could muster, I joined them in their tiny kitchen and was served a meal which went on endlessly. Soup, chilled sliced vegetables *vinaigrette, biftek grillé, poulet en sauce, tarte de pomme, fromage*, all accompanied by wines. The couple clearly didn't lunch like this every day. They were thin, elderly and poor. I knew this meal had been prepared especially for me while the man and woman raved on and on about the calves.

This was during the time of major coffee shortages all over the world (except perhaps in Brazil or Colombia). The French love their coffee strong and sweet. It was common to add chicory and, as coffee became scarcer and more expensive, the percentage of chicory to coffee increased. Believe me, it was bad. Enough to draw all the taste buds up and out the nasal passages.

The couple insisted I have a *tasse de café* before heading back out on the highway. Particularly after all the wine. I dutifully swigged back a mouthful of the wicked brew, discovered it to be 100 percent chicory, and only the sternest of self-disciplines forced it down my unwilling throat. After my previous perfidy, nothing would allow me to spew that mouthful of bitter black gunk all over my hostess' lovely table. I looked on it as penance.

I spent the entire drive home in self-flagellation. I could have lied cheerfully to any of the livestock dealers in the area and most of the farmers, but to have deliberately misled this sweet, elderly couple caused me enormous distress. If I could have corrected the situation short of turning around and admitting my criminal nature and buying back the calves, I would have done it. The bladder distress I suffered on the long way home from the fluids consumed at lunch seemed a small price to pay.

Right then I made a number of resolutions on handling business transactions and, for the next couple of years, remained steadfast, true and white-hatted. It was easy since my animals thrived.

It was at one of the local monthly market fairs in the village a few years later that I next saw the old couple. I tried to duck behind a display of kitchenware, but they had spotted me and trotted over, smiling and eager.

"Oh Madame, les vaches sont superbes!"
"Les meilleurs laitières de toutes!"

They bubbled over with superlatives on the two runtlings I'd sold them. The cows had apparently become prolific milk producers as well as being sweet, gentle pets. The old couple couldn't have been happier. They were recommending me to all their friends.

That was when guilt, cold and spike-edged, slithered right out of my heart and one good intention, soft and warm, oozed in to fill the gap, proving that they don't all wind up as paving stones. Sometimes good things happen.

Still, I don't think livestock dealing is my ideal profession.

❧ CHAPTER 36 ❧

Christmas Eve

Another Christmas season had arrived in the Dordogne. The final, golden tones of the organ died away in the stillness of the old stone church. I felt the approving sighs of long-departed organists from past centuries in the chill Christmas Eve air. Even more palpable was the relief issuing from the spirits of long-ago little boys who were responsible for pumping the bellows. With the electrification of the organ some sixty years ago, this was no longer a chore.

M'sieur and Madame Saint-Martin had visited one afternoon a few weeks earlier, exchanging *bonjours* and offering one of her superb *gateau aux noix*, which the kids would inhale right down to the plate. In no way am I implying that I wouldn't be right in the thick of the gourmet cake attack.

"Madame," M'sieur said slowly, then paused. It wasn't like him to be so hesitant. "Madame, we hear your wonderful piano from time to time. You play very well."

"Merci," I responded. "Perhaps I shouldn't leave the door open. I didn't realize the sound could travel that far."

"Oh, no, *je vous en prie, chère Madame.* But I...we... wondered," the hesitancy again, "do you also play the organ?"

Now it was my turn to hesitate. "Yes, when I was younger. I learned to play the organ in my church and then accompanied services for a little over a year."

"Mais, c'est formidable. You see, the organist who traditionally accompanies my solo at the Christmas Eve Mass is ill and unable to assist. If I am to sing, I must find an accompanist. Please say you will do it."

I was both honored and terrified at the thought of playing the sixteenth century organ in the village church at the Christmas Eve service. After eight years in Saint-Cyprien, I was still considered by many to be a vacationing tourist in spite of the fact that my children attended the village school and we sold milk from our dairy herd to the local buttery. My participation in a local event might signify my acceptance into the community.

I was nervous and excited at my first visit to the medieval church. The Saint-Martin's and I drove down our hillside to the village, then circled back up the other side. The old monastery had been a part of a chateau, built at the highest point for the best views of approaching marauders. The chateau was a semi-ruin, the monastery long-gone, but the church remained, its stone facade starkly beautiful, gazing protectively across the village to the river beyond, snaking in great curves through green pastures and plowed fields.

The massive door creaked open and we stepped in to the foyer, then turned left to a door that opened on narrow, curving, stone steps. It was necessary to stoop while ascending, organists apparently being much shorter back in the sixteenth century. The stone treads of the staircase were worn at the center from centuries of feet, like the wear on a rock canyon after millions of decades of God's breath blowing across.

"Magnifique!" I breathed. I was too in awe of my surroundings to speak aloud. The organ loft was at the rear of the church and my gaze was drawn along a long narrow nave toward the massive altar. The winter sun, which barely warmed the outside fields, shone through the stained glass windows behind the altar with a golden glow, as if the disciples depicted thereon radiated with the lights of heaven. The altar itself was a textured blend of velvety maroon cloths, golden oak and shining brass. The heavy brass pipes of the organ hung on alternate sides. Carved figures watched benevolently from alcoves along the side walls of the ancient edifice.

The large sanctuary was hushed and quiet, but not with solitude. An almost tangible Presence filled the air. Also a permeating, bone-chilling cold. No heat source had ever entered this building.

The organ dominated the small balcony, barely leaving space for M'sieur and Madame even after I scooted onto the bench. Images drifted through my mind of generations of organists who had played this venerable instrument and I felt insignificant and unworthy. M'sieur Saint-Martin had recounted stories of the master organists who traveled across Europe in ages past to play organs in *les eglises*. The old priest of *L'eglise de Saint-Cyprien*, had refused to let any other than certain "master" musicians play it, even if the alternative was for it to remain silent. To do otherwise, he believed, was sacrilege.

There was a new young priest, however, blowing fresh air through the ancient church—scandalizing some of the older parishioners, but bringing the young into the fold. I could hear him below in the sanctuary with a group of children, decorating the church for *Noël*. With hesitation, I ran through a couple of carols, "Silent Night," "Joy to the World," then switched to a simple Bach "Prelude." At first, my feet had trouble finding the pedals, but soon slipped into the old habits. Unfamiliar with the organ stops, I created some unusual and, to me, cacophonous sounds. M'sieur and Madame beamed and nodded. *"C'est bon! C'est bon!"*

Footsteps thudded up the stone stairway and the young priest popped into the small balcony, dancing around in the tiny space.

"Mais, c'est formidable!" he exclaimed. *"Magnifique* to have music for the service. You must play, *bien sûr,* as the people enter the church, then, of course, for the hymns, about fifteen minutes during communion and again as everyone leaves. *Magnifique!* It is so long since we have had music. *Un vrai ocasion de fête!"* He turned and bounced down the stone stairs, leaving the air charged with vibrant electricity and my mouth hanging open. So much for accompanying one simple solo.

I had about two weeks to re-learn old habits and become acquainted with—to me—a new organ. Not much time to learn which notes set off window vibrations or rattled the ancient pipes. But I worked hard, slipping into the tiny loft every afternoon and departing with inspirational thoughts and frozen hands, feet and nose.

I didn't have a whole lot of sheet music, but I found a book of Christmas carols and a book of Bach preludes. The majority of the carols so familiar to every American child, are unknown in France, but the joy and humble awe of the season sing out in each of them and I used them freely. I remembered old taboos against using secular music in the church, but somehow felt that He accepted the music in the spirit in which it was offered. Reverently. With love and gratitude.

On Christmas Eve, M'sieur Saint-Martin's baritone filled the church, mellow and sweet, as he sang the *Cantique de Noël*. When the parishioners had filed out and I was finished playing, I gathered my music and descended the stairs. The Saint-Martins had gone ahead to wish a *Joyeux Noël* to friends and to collect the car.

Jill, Jane and René were waiting in the foyer, along with a large group of villagers. *"C'etait vous? Mais, que c'etait beau!"* Was it really you? We didn't know you could play? It was *magnifique* to hear the organ again.

This Christmas Eve had accomplished great strides in international relations, in particular, Franco-American ones.

The Saint-Martins had invited Jane and René to join us for the traditional *reveillon*. I had Jill with me, but the older children had opted to spend the evening with friends, promising to be reasonable in their hour of returning. The term "reasonable" is open to many interpretations.

Madame retired to the kitchen to complete dinner preparations while M'sieur served aperitifs and it wasn't long before Madame was serving the *paté truffé* with great chunks of crusty bread. M'sieur and René discussed the merits of various wines, but agreed that a Saint-Emilion from the Bordeaux Valley would do nicely with the *canard roti*.

M'sieur Saint-Martin was a storyteller *extraordinaire* and the evening passed in a haze of exquisite food and excellent wine while he regaled us with the tale of the mysterious stranger who had restored the organ which I had just played.

The story contained everything, opening with the rapping on the monastery door on a dark and stormy night, the strange young man who claimed to be the son of a master organ artisan, begging to be allowed to restore the organ which had fallen into a terminal state of disrepair. The tale continued as the young man did odd jobs to earn money to buy the needed parts, working day and night, finally succeeding magnificently on a Christmas Eve much like this one and then disappearing once again into the chill mists of the Middle Ages.

M'sieur could really weave a tale and we believed every word he spoke. On the other hand, after a couple of glasses of Saint Emilion, I'll fall for almost anything.

My sleepy daughter and I arrived home after a magical evening and found the others tucked in their beds. I stood for a while gazing at the stars glittering brightly in the frosty sky. I wondered which one might have shone over a stable in Bethlehem.

My heart was filled with thankfulness, for my children, for good and loving friends, for music. But my teeth were chattering with cold and I headed toward flannel sheets, piles of blankets, a multitude of cats and a warm puppy.

CHAPTER 37

Farewell

"Mais oui, Madame, c'est dommage mais c'est comme ça." (It's a shame, but that's how it is.) The principal of the local school, whom I had come to know well over the past ten years, was confirming the fact that acceptance to the French universities was based on grades—grades of French students, from the top right down to those barely capable of spelling their names. Then, any remaining spaces could be filled by the very top foreign students. If any spaces remained. Most doubtful.

Throughout their school careers all these years, the kids had been at the tops of their classes. Grades were not a problem. Nationality was. And career opportunities after university, assuming that obstacle could be overcome, were another problem.

The time had come to consider our future, especially my children's future opportunities. Life in Oz appeared to be no longer practical.

The children and I carefully listed the pros and cons. The fact that I loved my life here was pitifully lonesome on the pro list. The cons weighed much heavier. Once again, it was time for a family vote. The older ones were enthusiastic about moving to Arizona, where their grandparents and miscellaneous aunts, uncles and cousins waited to receive us. There, university and career opportunities were ripe for the plucking. I, with deep regret, had to join in their vote. Only Jill, still too young to deal with hard, cold facts and with a teenager's tunnel vision, voted vehemently to stay. My heart joined her.

Memories kaleidoscoped in my thoughts, melding our ten years in France into one unbroken reverie:

The morning I looked into the field below the barn at the cows grazing the dew-soaked grass and noticed a doe and fawn stepping daintily from the woods to join them. Peaceful companions until startled by a noise, a scent, then with fluid grace they soared over the fence and disappeared soundlessly, instantly, back into the woods. The yearlings gazed in open-mouthed wonder, unchewed grass hanging in clumps from their lips. Bovine brains at work, they galloped clumsily at the fence and lurched into it in their attempt at flight, the first in line bearing the brunt of the electric current and bellowing pain and puzzlement.

The day Lily, our *vache normandaise,* zealously guarded the cider apples from the trees bordering the lane, as the herd munched on alfalfa too sparse for a second cutting. Running off her sisters, she gobbled down every apple on the ground as well as those still clinging to low branches, whether green or nearly ripe. Then, moaning in pain as her stomach swelled with the inevitable fermentation. Ah, for a cow-sized Tums!

The time I returned to find my teenaged sons with two friends using the hose to shoo off an indignant Petunia from the kitchen door, which the turkey was valiantly defending against all invasion, even family. It took my arrival, his beloved "mom," for him to shake the water dripping from his black plumage and grudgingly allow them entry.

A frosty morning with a whiff of smoke on the air, each blade of grass cocooned in ice, errant breezes through frozen leaves sounding like fragile wind chimes as the cows stomped for entry, with steam rising from their bodies and icicles like streamers on horns and eyelashes.

The barn was filled from beam to beam, covering even the pigeon holes, with fresh hay, smelling of open fields and sweat. The bin in the *grenier* was topped with barley, bags of corn still remained from last year's harvest, the livestock were fat, sleek and sassy.

I no longer felt like an unloved castoff. I'd been told by Rob I was traded for someone "a lot like me." I wondered what the difference was. Whatever. I was whole now; my therapy complete.

Along the way, I'd worked and learned. Struggled, sweated, cried and laughed. Some days my toenails ached from hanging on. But, by damn! we'd hung in and, today, we were sitting on top of the branch. Well, at least, we had a good armhold. Maybe this was a good time to prepare for the next phase of our lives.

We started planning our return to the States a year in advance. A year to sell the livestock and equipment, to sell the property, find homes for the pets, make decisions, inform friends. It was tough.

Winter is the time when the giant tobacco stalks, which have been hanging in drying sheds and barns, must be taken down, the leaves stripped and divided into bundles by size. It's a time when families and friends—you've got to be a really good friend to do this—get together in cold, drafty barns to work together and talk to keep their minds off the fact their toes are about to freeze right off their feet.

Jane and René and I usually worked with the Gorse and Groliére family whose farm lay between *Vezat* and *Saint Pompon*. Their property was split by *La Route de Sinzelle,* and it was not at all uncommon for cars or farm equipment to stop and wait for a mama duck and her brood to cluck their way across. The elder Groliéres owned the land and when their daughter married Marcellou Gorse, he joined them. By the time of our arrival at *Vezat*, there was a third generation, a boy and girl, all working together.

They had a spring that bubbled up beside the road, bordered by a low rock wall where, weekly, the women pounded out laundry. Madame Groliére insisted proudly that no machine would ever wad up and destroy her fine linen sheets. When she pounded the wash, *mon Dieu!*, she knew it was clean.

M'sieur Groliére rivaled René with his collection of tales about the neighborhood and its occupants. While our fingers were busily separating the dry papery leaves from the stalks, they told stories as we laughed, Marcellou interjecting from time to time his own bits of dry wit. It was mid-afternoon and the last of the stalks was in sight when René asked me if I would get to do this in Arizona.

"Qu'est-ce que c'est que ça? Arizona? What will she be doing in Arizona?" M'sieur Groliére jumped on the comment in an instant.

"I, we...we're moving back. For the children, you know,"
I didn't know how to explain.

"But you can't. You can't." The old man smiled at me,
friend to friend. "You're one of us."

It was the finest compliment I'd ever received.

My insurance agent was also in the real estate business
and I spoke with him about the property. And received the
shock of my life. All the while I had been fencing, haying, planting, reaping and going about daily living, the property had
been shooting upward in value. The value he wanted to place
on the farm was over three times the price we had paid for it
slightly less than ten years earlier.

The first client he brought to see our farm was a
woman, very chic, very blonde, very rich, accompanied by her
ranch manager. She had inherited an *elevage des veaux* and
wanted to expand the operation. She appeared to look favorably on the fields, found them *acceptable*, referred to the buildings as *ruines* and stated her intention to bulldoze them and
rebuild.

To be perfectly honest, I wouldn't have liked anyone
who bought *Vezat*. In addition, it was okay for us to refer to our
beloved home as a ruin; it was insulting coming from her. The
final knife in the wound was the thought of our farm with its
contented animals becoming a place where calves were cruelly
raised to become slabs of chemically-induced white meat.

I refused her offer.

This, obviously, wasn't going to work. Business dealings
must be made through rational thought. Not emotions.

Once again, M'sieur Charbonnel provided the answer.
He came with his son Luc, now grown and recently married, to
discuss their proposal. Luc had married an only child, daughter
of a dairy farmer, and was expanding the operation. He made

an offer for my entire dairy herd. He and his father together wanted to lease the *Vezat* property to add to the adjoining fields below and double the capacity for beef cattle. They requested a three-year lease with annual options for renewal.

The dark clouds lifted, the barometric pressure on my heart lightened and the first birds of spring sang softly. Sometimes, I'd found, decisions need to be pushed back until they can be made without emotional baggage. That which can't be borne now, can be faced later.

"I'll think about it tomorrow," Scarlet said, shutting the door. I adopted her strategy hoping that, when tomorrow came, I'd be ready—at least partially—to do what had to be done.

As the time for our departure crept closer, we were left with only the family pets. Homes were found for the cats; *Trompette* would feel right at home in Gabriel's hutches since he'd spent a large portion of his life with the *lapines* there already; Vicky was going to learn English in Arizona with us; Penny was buried in our little animal graveyard next to her little friend, Schultz; and then there was Jerry.

Jerry. We considered taking him with us. However, the cost and difficulty of transport were prohibitive and, with his heavy mountain coat of fur, we doubted his ability to survive in the desert climate.

René brought an older couple to us who lived along the river road to Belvès. They were sympathetic, assuring us that Jerry would be in a large fenced yard and would be loved and cared for. René spoke of them favorably. We packed a bag with our dog's bowls and brush, hugged him and he, always happy to ride in a car, stuffed himself into the back seat and drove off with the couple, head and tongue lolling out the back window.

"C'est bien. Eh oui, c'est bien," muttered René.

We nodded through lumpy throats and dripping tears.

Three mornings later, Gabriel rattled into the lane announcing that the owner of the tractor repair shop along the river road reported seeing a big white dog trotting toward the village just after dawn. Sure enough, an hour later, Jerry, tired but ecstatic, slurped down a bowl of water and flopped happily in the doorway to survey his kingdom.

René joined me in a visit to the couple on the river road. Sure enough, they had a lovely large yard enclosed in a chain-link fence. We looked at the corner where the wire had been ripped from the post. I couldn't imagine how he did it. The man and woman assured us it would be repaired and strengthened, they truly wanted the *gros chien*, please give them another chance. I agreed with deep misgivings.

This time it took him only two days. René chugged in on his *mobylette* at noon to say Jerry had been seen during the morning. Gabriel arrived shortly thereafter with the great hound stuffed amongst the tools and debris in his car.

"Found him on the road. He looked tired," he chuckled.

Jerry didn't look tired to me. Mischief gleamed in the dark eyes as he slathered me with kisses. I hugged the huge beast.

After a great deal of thought, I ran an advertisement in the Perigueux newspaper, offering him for sale. A week later we had a call from a young couple living on a small farm in the mountains many miles from Saint-Cyprien. When they drove in, two small children, a girl and boy, perhaps six and eight, hopped out of the car and within minutes were patting and playing with Jerry. The parents were people I would have enjoyed counting as friends, serious but with ready smiles, hard-working. They assured me their property was well fenced.

The way Jerry was looking at the children, I thought they might be an even better source of enclosure.

We agreed, shook hands and the young man reached into his pocket for a worn wallet and pulled out some bills. I refused.

"Mais, pourquoi?" he asked, puzzled.

"I just wanted to make sure you knew he had value," I said. "I think you know. Your kids know." Then I added, "I can't sell a family member."

Our last sight of Jerry was with two children entwined in the heavy white fur as he cast a final, laughing glance through the back window. I think he knew. And accepted.

One last thing remained to be done. I went into the hay barn, filled with the year's hay for the Charbonnel cattle. No longer mine. I reached into my pocket and removed the knife that I had discovered many years before and placed it on the old hutches, pulling a scrap of hay over it. It belonged there.

The three older children left first on a charter flight from Paris, available only to students. The price for their fares was extremely reasonable and, other than a delay in Paris due to striking air traffic controllers, the trip was uneventful.

Jill, Vicky and I were taking the night train to Paris. *Au revoirs* and *adieus* had been said. The farm was empty of life except for a few wild bantam chickens perched in the trees. Even the night sounds were muted in the summer air.

Jane and René drove us to the train. We didn't talk much, there was too much on our hearts. Promises were made to write, to visit soon. Last hugs.

The train was nearly empty. No one with any sense or any other choice traveled this way, with stops at every village along the four-hundred-mile route. The milk run. We had a compartment to ourselves. Jill, exhausted from the long day, but even more by the emotional toll, stretched out and was soon asleep. Vicky curled tightly into my lap, her own personal security blanket.

The train clickety-clacked through the night, slowing and stopping at darkened stations, then moving on. I watched the passing of villages and shadows through a mist of tears, joy and regret blending and blurring. The Land of Oz was being left behind and I was returning to the real world. Or was it the other way around?

I'd arrived in France a much different person—more naïve, perhaps, more trusting. A wife and mother following my husband's desire for adventure, but somewhere over time, that adventure became mine.

The children had been small when we'd left the States; they were growing into young men and women with a broad base of cultures to carry forward into their adult lives. There were still years of schooling ahead, years in which to re-affirm their character and integrity. I was proud of what they'd accomplished.

For me, I had tackled an unknown world, wrestled it to the ground and, although I couldn't say I'd pinned it to the mat, I'd held my own. Almost a decade ago, my self-confidence had been ripped apart and left in tattered shreds. A future that seemed to spread before me, as certain as my mother's and her mother's before her, had disintegrated like dandelion puff.

The first time I'd gazed into a barn, filled to the rafters with sweet-smelling hay knowing that every morsel had been grown on my fields, cut, raked and gathered by my own efforts, it hadn't mattered that it was stacked slightly precariously, that

the bales weren't exactly squared off. What had been important was that the beasts in my care, grazing in the fields of
Vezat, would be as fat and sleek at the end of winter as they
were in spring and summer, when the fields were thick with
rich grasses. The cows, the orphaned sheep, dogs, cats, ducks
and miscellaneous critters that quacked and peeped and
squawked. And needed me. My self-esteem had picked itself up,
blown off specks of hay and dust and ever-so-slightly puffed
itself up.

Quite possibly it was learning to speak and think in
another language that made the difference. One's concepts
change. The central core shifts. Or maybe it was the difference
in the people, the emphasis on family and friends, less on
plumbing and possessions.

These years had allowed me the luxury of drawing the
tatty rags of my rejection around me, hiding away from a world
which might have judged me wanting or unworthy, until I
could return with my head up and no apology. I felt like
Christopher Columbus or Marco Polo. I stopped a little short of
Alexander the Great or Attila the Hun. I came, I saw. It might be
a bit presumptuous to say I conquered. But I certainly survived.
I'd even go so far as to say I did better than maintain the status
quo.

I learned. I laughed. I had a whole new corps of dear
friends. I could do masses of things undreamed of in my prior
life. Memories lay warm and tender upon my heart.

It was time now to do it all over again.

PART 4

Apres Tout

You robed yourself in fog
when first we met,
A drenching rain obscured your face.
We wept.

Your barns were filled with
decades of dried dung,
Your rooms with crusted soot and grime and shame.
We moaned.

You opened yourself to me
like a lover,
baring your sun soaked fields,
your enchanted woods of oak and juniper and holly.
Your shades remembered
men who strode your turf,
not in armor with swords

but homespun and scythes,
your princesses without satin or lace
but cotton and sturdy shoes,
who dreamed.

Your walls unwired,
your floors unplumbed,
yet magic in a hidden spring
gushing iced ambrosia watercress-bordered.
A cherry tree with too-late fruit and too-soon wrens
who laughed.

You filled my soul with seasons,
Heartbeats of forgotten time.
Gleeful winds and storms of manic temper,
Summer rains on drying hay.
I lived.

❧ CHAPTER 38 ❧

And After

Here we were, back in America, home of big cars, fast foods and Pillsbury croissants, temporarily ensconced and definitely pushing out the walls of my brother-in-law's home. Me, a batch of unwieldy teenagers (the youngest still firmly refusing to speak English) and a dog that understood only French. The brother-in-law was Rob's brother and his wife was Pat, my dearest friend and sender of CARE packages. Bearing in mind the comparison between house guests and cheese and how neither improves with the passage of time, I had to rent us a place to live soon. Landlords, however, have this strange preference for employed tenants. Hence, the need to find a job.

And that was the problem. For the last ten years, I'd been a dairy farmer in southwestern France. The toughest part of the whole ten-year experience was finding a job when it was over. I mean, how does one prepare a resumé when milking cows has been your occupation for the past

ten years? I figured I could put "Farm Management" under
Job Title, but for Duties and Responsibilities "Milking cows
and shoveling shit" just didn't seem to be qualifications for
legal secretary. Well, shoveling shit perhaps, but not milking
cows.

On the plus side, I thought, at least it showed job sta-
bility. During the ten years before that, I'd given birth to four
kids and changed a gazillion diapers, been a Girl Scout leader,
directed a pre-teen handbell choir, given piano lessons to kids
who slept with their baseball mitts and been a Little League
car pool driver. That made a total of twenty years since I'd last
filed a tort or prepared a contract. Twenty years to gloss over
and convince a prospective employer that the time in France
was all actively utilized in honing skills and enhancing my
value in the job market.

My first interview was a disaster. I arrived wearing the
skirt and blouse I'd thought appropriate and neat black
pumps with two-inch heels. The skirt was new, since my
wardrobe consisted entirely of hand-me-down jeans (from
my sons) or a pair of wool slacks (for dress-up). The shoes
were also new, my options consisting of rubber boots or
sneakers, but I'd neglected to take into account re-learning to
walk in them.

I walked into an office with ten acres of polished
mahogany desk. Behind it sat a man wearing a charcoal suit,
complete with vest, and a muted mauve tie. He raised his
rump briefly when I entered, reached across the acreage to
shake hands as I juggled tucking in my blouse with one hand
and clutching purse and resumé with the other. Settling for
waving me to the chair, he gazed unhappily at my greying
hair, pulled into a neat ponytail, and scrubbed face and

turned his attention to the application I shoved across the shining surface of the desk.

"Well, now." His attention was caught by my non run-of-the-mill background. "What took you to France? Husband in the military?"

Any damn fool ought to know that the United States hadn't had bases in France for thirty years. I didn't really want to go into detail on this subject so I murmured something about seeking a drug-free, back-to-nature environment for the children and let it go. But he didn't want to let it go; I'd caught his interest. Damn!

"So, tell me a bit about it. What was the farm like and what, exactly, did you do?"

And there I sat, like a naïve idiot, trying to discreetly rub the cramp in my left calf, telling this man who specialized in bleeding insurance companies dry for maximum legal fees and minimum client benefits the story of the farm in France. I waxed eloquent over the emerald green fields bordered with ancient oak woods, with their russet-plumed pheasant and twittering grouse, glossed over the three-hundred-year old ruins and spoke with affection of my herd of placid milk cows and obstreperous calves. His eyes grew wide as he said, "What courage."

Courage? It was an attribute I hadn't considered I possessed. I hadn't had time to ponder such things. Stupidity I had. In spades. Stupid to believe a husband who spouted the advantages of the "Simple Life" then suggested the children and I go on ahead to France and establish residency and get started in school while he stayed behind in the States to arrange the sale of a faltering business. Stupid when, even after two years with a couple of short visits per year, I failed to recognize that he had deposited his family in a faraway, pastoral paradise and had returned to the States not to settle his affairs, but rather to live with her.

My interviewer said he felt my qualifications didn't quite fulfill their requirements, wished me well and I limped out of the office on swollen feet.

I regarded my second interview as a fact-finding mission. The man seated at a similar massive and shining desk was wearing an identical suit and vest as the first one, this time with a tie of muted pea-soup green. The receptionist who admitted me to the great man's presence was tiny and lissome with enormous blue eyes, faultless make-up and short curly hair. She wore four-inch spike heels with tiny straps and her long, glistening, crimson-polished nails had never been near a typewriter.

I answered his questions briefly without going into detail, heard the inevitable, "Was your husband in the military?" and eventually the "I *do* wish you luck but, unfortunately..." and I was out the door rubbing the screaming cramp in my left leg and stuffing in that damn shirttail. I glanced at the office next to his and heard the hum of electronics and saw the female worker bees, middle-aged, but attractive and professional-looking. The next day I made an appointment at a beauty shop recommended by my sister-in-law.

For ten years, I'd created a life bounded by seasons. A winter freeze which broke newly installed water pipes in the old house and created an ice sculpture spouting from under the eaves. False springs in February with two or three perfect weeks of sun followed by freezing rains in March and April. A summer filled with haying, of *fêtes de foin* shared with friends and neighbors, of barley and corn harvests leading to the grandest event of all, the *vendage*, the grape harvest into the great *cuves* which ferment the year's production of wine. I recalled the cows entering the milking barn in winter with icicles festooning their horns and eyelashes or sloshing through the spring muds; a newborn calf struggling, wetly, to its feet and unerringly finding the dangling *tetine* while the mother's brown eyes glowed with the love and pride of mothers of all species.

My thoughts turned to Gabriel, his beret perched jauntily on his head, insouciantly teaching us how to farm, reveling in our ignorance. In comparison to us, he was a master of the art. He soon discovered our love of needy animals and regularly deposited the sick and orphaned on our doorstep. A huge dog, a tiny puppy, hours-old lambs orphaned at birth and left on the manure pile to die were handed over as gifts in exchange for *un coup de rouge*. How I would miss him!

Nevertheless, it was time to face the fact that I had returned. The Land of Oz disappeared once again into the mists. I needed to learn to live once again in my own land, my own time.

I hit the library and spent hours researching the law, re-acquainting myself with the terminology, with the endless variations of forms and procedures. I prowled the malls and studied fashions. I worked on that all-important resumé and, when I received a request for another interview, I was ready.

My resumé, professionally prepared on creamy, textured bond, was a symphony of the double entendre, in the words of Shakespeare, "all sound and fury and signifying nothing." Under Farm Management, the Duties and Responsibilities included such administrative tasks as Coordinating legal documents with regulatory authorities (residency permits),

Contract negotiations with local building contractors (getting a septic tank installed), Building maintenance (mucking out barns) and Animal husbandry (there's the milking). For my next interview, I walked into an office with a gigantic expanse of desk and the requisite distinguished executive in his three-piece suit and dove-gray tie. I was wearing a simple tailored dress with one-inch heeled pumps (muscle development takes time). My hair was short and softly curled, tinted brown with chestnut highlights. My eyes and lips were lightly touched with the latest from Revlon. I entered the room confidently, just as if I knew what I was doing, shook hands across the polished surface, extracted my masterpiece from a professional portfolio and waited for the usual questions.

They were not forthcoming. He glanced briefly at the document and started discussing his practice, inquiring into my familiarity with estate law. He sang the intricacies of Revocable Living Trusts and I harmonized sweetly with durable Powers of Attorney, Trust Officers and Living Wills.

I got the job. Which all goes to prove that silk purses can be created out of sow's ears, but I'll always believe that the ears look better on the sow.

That job led, in time, to another job, a better one at Arizona State University from which my son, Dan, later graduated with a degree in Electrical Engineering and where I met my new husband.

All the kids are now grown and independent. Actually, they were pretty independent even back then. Perhaps it's in the genes.

Wendy married her high school sweetheart and I have a French granddaughter. Dan designs computer microchips. Tim discovered a gift for languages and a love of travel and runs a language school in Indonesia. Jill and her family, including two sons, live very near me.

I dream a lot. Always have. I hope I always will. When stress piles up, when joy is beaten down under everyday problems, I often find myself drifting in sleep to that spot under the oak in the big field. The stars in an inky sky slide past the trees and minuet across infinity. I hear the cows ruminating, a rabbit skids to a halt in the field and sits upright, whiskers twitching, then decides I pose no danger and resumes his search for clover, tasting, nibbling.

The earth smells of fresh cut grass, essence of cow, impending rain. Something skitters through the leafy bed of the woods behind me, stops, rustles again. The owl calls softly, "Who?"

Vezat and the Valley of the Dordogne are deeply imprinted in our souls and hearts. Olga and Petula, Babette and Nicky, Petunia, Jerry and the dogs we left buried under the old walnut tree, ChiChi and the generations of cats, the good friends and the seasons of work and play, joy and sorrow, tears and laughter will live forever in our memories.